LOVE GRATITUDE HOPE
GRACE HAPPINESS
HOPE CO
FAITH WISDOM
PEACE FAITH LOVE
LOVE GRATITUDE HOPE
HOPE COMFORT FAITH WI
OM JESUS P
RT G
TH CE GRACE COMFORT HOPE CO
ATITUDE WISDOM JOY GU
OPE FAITH JOY LOVE
ESS GUIDANCE PEACE HA
GRA
E GRACE FAITH J
RATITUDE LOVE TI
COMFORT JOY HAPPI
GUIDANCE FAITH
E TIME GRACE JOY LO
HAPPINESS HOPE GRAC

DANCE PEACE GRACE FAITH
E TIME LOVE GRATITU
HAPPINESS HOPE COMFOR
ACE WISDOM JOY GUIDANC
MFORT LOVE TIME
PEACE JOY LOVE HAPPINES
HAPPINESS GRACE WISD
E GUIDANCE PEACE COMF
Y GRATITUDE JOY FA
GRACE HAPPINESS PEA
OPE COMFORT HOPE G
WISDOM GRACE GRATITUDE
ACE TIME LOVE HAPP
RATITUDE HOPE TI
HO
OY LOVE TIME LOVE G
PEACE HAPPINESS PEAC
GRACE WISDOM J
H GRATITUDE
JOY LO
ISDOM FAITH

TO:

Lauren

FROM:

Archu and Benny

Much love! Happy Mother's
Day!

JESUS, I NEED YOU

DEVOTIONS

From Your Heart to His

ZONDERVAN®

Cover design: Connie Gabbert
Interior design: Mallory Perkins

ISBN-13: 978-0-310-34392-9

Printed in China

15 16 17 18 19 TIMS 6 5 4 3 2

CONTENTS

JESUS,
I NEED
YOUR . . .

GUIDANCE

1

I NEED YOU

Dear Jesus,

Sometimes I forget just how much I need You. How many times have You tried to tell me something, and I haven't listened? I need to listen more. How often have You tried to show me something, but I haven't seen? I need to open my eyes to every little blessing. I need to take time to look up at the sky and down at the earth and recognize the amazing work of the Father's hands. I need to see into the hearts of others so I can sympathize and empathize with them and be a servant to them more often.

Dear Jesus, I need You. Every day, every minute, every second, I need You. Teach me to seek You more every day. Remind me that unless I take time to draw near to You, I will have trouble hearing Your voice and seeing what You want me to see. Jesus, when I read my Bible, reveal Yourself to me. Show me all the ways I need You. Fill up my heart, spare me from the world's distractions, and help me focus on You.

I need You.

And my God will meet all your needs according to the riches of his glory in Christ Jesus.—Philippians 4:19

We all need a Savior. We all need Jesus. Not only did He save us from our sins and provide our way to heaven, but Jesus wants to save us from anything that gets in the way of our relationship with Him. He wants to fill up your heart with His love. You need Him.

....

....

....

....

....

....

....

....

....

....

....

....

....

....

....

....

....

....

2

SCATTERED THOUGHTS

Dear Jesus,

My thoughts are so scattered today. The anxiety that comes with too many things to do and getting them all done makes my mind spin out of control. I'm having trouble reeling in my thoughts and organizing them so that I can think clearly and set a productive plan.

Lord, instead of concentrating on my work, I've let what-ifs and if-onlies sneak into my head. What if I can't do this? or What if I can't get it done on time? If only I didn't have so much to do! If only I had someone to help me! But I do have Someone to help me—Jesus, I have You!

Why can't I remember to call on You first? You are always with me and ready to help. So help me now, Lord Jesus. Remove those what-ifs and if-onlies from my brain. Gather my thoughts like God gathers the four corners of the wind. Bring them all together—organized, ready, and clear.

Jesus, You are my Helper. Together, we'll get this done.

We demolish arguments and every pretension that sets itself up against the knowledge of God, and we take captive every thought to make it obedient to Christ.—2 Corinthians 10:5

When burdened with so much to do, your thoughts can become anxious and tangled. That's when you need to lean on Jesus. He knows how to calm you, help you sort through all of the mismatched thoughts, and organize them to get the work done. Call on Him in your busiest times. He is ready and willing to help.

....

....

....

....

....

....

....

....

....

....

....

....

....

....

....

....

....

....

3

GIVING IT ALL AWAY

Dear Jesus,

I have a confession to make. I feel afraid to entrust every-thing to You. I know that You love me and want only the best for me. Still, it's so hard to give up total control of every aspect of my life. When I have trouble, I'm eager to give You my problems. But when things are going well, I'm not as quick to give my every-thing away.

My concern, Jesus, is not knowing. If I give you my every-thing, I want to know what You plan to do with it. Will You make big changes? You know that I don't do well with change. Will there be valleys along the way and mountains to climb?

I should just trust You. I want to trust You. Why is trust so hard? I pray, dear Jesus, that You will help me with this. Teach me that I needn't be afraid. Help me give You my everything—just maybe not all at once. Take my hand and lead me gently, one step at a time.

"For I know the plans I have for you,"
declares the Lord, "plans to prosper you
and not to harm you, plans to give you
hope and a future."—Jeremiah 29:11

Handing over everything to God can be difficult, especially for those who have been hurt by someone they love. It is important to remember that God is perfect Love. Because He loved us, He gave us His everything—His only Son. Jesus suffered for us so that we will have eternal life in heaven one day. Learn to trust Him. He loves you.

....

....

....

....

....

....

....

....

....

....

....

....

....

....

....

....

....

4
TEMPTATION

Dear Jesus,

Why is self-control so difficult? Whether it's about overeating, spending too much time on the computer, or losing my temper, I sometimes give in to temptation and do what I know is wrong.

I tell myself, "Jesus was tempted, and He didn't give in." And then I remind myself that You are perfect, and I'm not. Oh, how I wish I were perfect and didn't have to struggle with right and wrong.

Jesus, the only way to overcome temptation and maintain my self-control is to keep my eyes on You and remember Your example. You were prepared when Satan tempted You. You knew that tempting might happen, and You were ready. I need to be ready, like You. I need to be ready and face temptation with Your kind of strength, the strength that comes with trusting God. I need to arm myself with Scripture, like You did, so I can fight off those tempting thoughts. When I feel like giving in, I have to remember to stop and ask You to help me.

Jesus, You are always with me. You fill the gaps of my imperfection with Your perfection. Lord Jesus, I trust You. Let's work on this together.

Because he himself suffered when he was
tempted, he is able to help those who
are being tempted.—Hebrews 2:18

Temptation is all around us, but Jesus taught us how to over-come it by setting a perfect example. Read Matthew 4:1–11. You will see that Jesus was prepared; He stayed strong and used God's Word to overcome the enemy. If you'll put His example into practice, You can overcome temptation too.

....

....

....

....

....

....

....

....

....

....

....

....

....

....

....

....

....

....

....

5
ON PRAYER

Dear Jesus,

Forgive me. I noticed today that I've been giving You instructions when I pray. You know what I want, and You also know what I need. But when I've prayed, I've told You exactly how I think You should answer my prayer. I've laid my plans before You and asked You to bless them, forgetting that prayer doesn't work that way.

Jesus, I am so used to being in control. It's my job to control things at home and at work to make sure that everything runs smoothly. I'm sorry that I've tried to control You.

You know better than I how to answer my prayer. You know whether to say yes to me, or no. And if you say no, then I can be certain that Your plan is a better one.

I want to pray in accordance with Your will, Jesus, but sometimes I get ahead of myself. Forgive me.

Many are the plans in a person's heart, but it is the Lord's purpose that prevails.—Proverbs 19:21

If anyone knew about prayer, it was Corrie ten Boom, the famous Dutch woman who was imprisoned for helping Jews escape the Nazis during WWII. About prayer she said, "It is not our task to give God instructions. We are simply to report for duty."[1] Prayer is not only about asking but also about listening. Make your needs known to the Lord, but then trust Him to answer in His own time and way.

....

....

....

....

....

....

....

....

....

....

....

....

....

....

....

....

....

....

6
JESUS, MY HELPER

Dear Jesus,

There are some things that I'm just not good at—numbers, for instance. When I have to balance my checkbook or do just about any kind of math, I freeze. I've never been good with numbers and I make mistakes. And cooking? I'm not so good at that either, or with creative things like drawing and writing. But, Jesus, the good news is that I keep on trying, and slowly I'm getting better at the things that I find difficult to do.

I'm learning relax and turn my thought processes over to You. You help me to think more clearly. You've taught me to take tasks slowly, one step at a time. When I trust in Your help, You give me hope that I can accomplish what I set out to do. When I make You my partner in a difficult task, then I am confident. There is nothing that You and I can't do together!

So thank You, Jesus. Thank You for being my helper.

I lift up my eyes to the mountains—
where does my help come from? My help
comes from the LORD.—Psalm 121:1–2

When you face a difficult task, call on Jesus for help. His wisdom will guide you. Ask Him to lead your thoughts and to help you focus on what you need to get done. If you make Jesus your partner, then you will see your self-confidence begin to flourish. He will help you stay calm and keep trying when you feel like giving up.

....

....

....

....

....

....

....

....

....

....

....

....

....

....

....

....

....

....

7

I SURRENDER ALL

Dear Jesus,

How many times have I laid everything at Your feet: my problems, my hopes, my prayers, and my life? I surrendered it all to You and then I took it all back. And, Jesus, I did it without one ounce of awareness. My need to be in control is so fundamental that I don't even recognize when I'm doing it.

Lord, I trust You. I am willing to hand over my everything to You, and I believe that You will take it and use it for my good and Your glory. Still, I am so often impatient waiting for Your solutions to my problems or answers to my prayers. When I'm impatient, I react impulsively. I've taken back what I've given You—and for that, dear Jesus, I am sorry!

Please help me. Once more, I surrender it all to You. And Jesus, I don't want it back. Help me leave it all with You, forever.

"Truly I tell you," Jesus replied, "no one who has left home or brothers or sisters or mother or father or children or fields for me and the gospel will fail to receive a hundred times as much in this present age."—Mark 10:29–30

Judson Van DeVenter struggled with surrendering all to Jesus. He wavered between his dream of becoming an accomplished artist and God's plan for him to enter the ministry. Finally, Judson made the choice to leave his dream with Jesus. The result? He became a powerful evangelist and hymnist. Perhaps you know his most famous hymn, "I Surrender All."[2] What might the Lord do with your life if you surrender all to Him?

....

....

....

....

....

....

....

....

....

....

....

....

....

....

....

....

8

GUIDE ME AND MY CHILDREN

Dear Jesus,

From the day my children were born, I've prayed for them to grow strong in faith and follow You all the days of their lives.

When they were little, it was easy. I read them Bible stories and we sang worship songs together. In Sunday school they learned about You and the sacrifice You made so that we can be together in heaven someday. But as my children are growing older, I see rebellion creeping into their hearts. They are increasingly tempted to follow their peers instead of You, and that frightens me.

I do my best to guide them, but I need Your help, Jesus. Root Yourself firmly in their hearts. Speak to them in ways that I cannot. Lead them to friends who love You, and guide them toward pleasing You instead of those who want to lead them astray.

And guide me also! I want a good, God-centered relationship with my children, one filled with love and trust. Show me if someone or something is taking Your place in their hearts, and teach me how to lead them back to You. Bless my children, Lord, and keep them close to You.

Start children off on the way they should go, and even when they are old they will not turn from it. —Proverbs 22:6

Charles Spurgeon said, "A child's back must be made to bend, but it must not be broken. He must be ruled, but not with a rod of iron. His spirit must be conquered, but not crushed."[3] *But how do I do that?* you wonder. The most important thing you will ever do for your children is to guide them into a strong Christian faith. Keep your eyes on Jesus and ask Him to help you. He will.

....

....

....

....

....

....

....

....

....

....

....

....

....

....

....

....

9

DECISIONS

Dear Jesus,

First, I want to thank You for blessing me. You have set before me two very attractive paths, and I'm grateful for that. But, Jesus, deciding which one to take is so hard. I've been praying about it, but so far I haven't felt You steer me in one way or the other. Tell me, please: What should I do?

I've thought hard about it. Both paths have benefits for my family and me, but each leads us in a very different direction. Each is quite different from the life we live now. I want to do what's right and what's best for us, not only now, but in the future.

I need Your wisdom and guidance. I've searched Your Word looking for direction, and I've prayed. Now I need You to speak to me. I can't stay stuck in this place of indecision, and my time to decide is running out. Tell me, dear Jesus. Which should I choose?

> *Blessed are those who find wisdom,*
> *those who gain understanding. . . . Her*
> *ways are pleasant ways, and all her*
> *paths are peace.* —Proverbs 3:13, 17

When faced with a tough decision, it is always important to pray for guidance and to search the Bible for answers. But what should you do when you ask the Lord to help you decide and He is silent? Sometimes God leaves the decision up to you. Remember, He already knows which path you will choose. And He promises in Proverbs 3:6 that if you keep your eyes fixed on Him, He will direct your paths.

....

....

....

....

....

....

....

....

....

....

....

....

....

....

....

....

10
LIGHT MY WAY

Dear Jesus,

I am like a ship lost at sea. Lonely, I search through this dark night looking for a welcoming beacon on shore. I need the light that is You. I need You to guide me home.

You know that I have been drifting without direction. So, Jesus, find me when I pray. Guide me through the pages of Your Word and enlighten me. Help me regain my faith and to trust in You once more.

My belief has been shaken, Lord, but I don't want to give up on You. I know that You have not left me—I have left You! The truth is that I am weak and You are strong, so strong that Your ways are beyond my understanding. Right now, all that is human in me feels raw and abandoned.

Sweet Jesus, guide me back to You. Restore my relationship with You, because that is the only thing that will give me peace.

Search me, God, and know my heart; test me and know my anxious thoughts. See if there is any offensive way in me, and lead me in the way everlasting.—Psalm 139:23-24

Has some event left you questioning Your faith? When a Christian feels apart from Jesus, it is a lonely feeling. If you find yourself in this situation, dig deep into God's Word and spend a lot of time in meditation and prayer. Ask God to search your heart and remove any barrier that is between you and Him. Trust Him to guide you back to your faith.

REFLECTIONS ON GUIDANCE

REFLECTIONS ON GUIDANCE

JESUS, I NEED YOU . . .

WHEN I FEEL OVERWHELMED

1

I CAN'T DO IT MYSELF

Dear Jesus,

I believe by faith that You are with me, but sometimes You seem so far away. I'm tired, weary, and overwhelmed by my obligations. Everyone wants a part of me, and I have nothing left to give. I'm trying to please everyone, encourage and support them, love them. I put forth my best effort, and all I feel is frustrated and alone.

Sometimes I feel like shouting, "Don't you know that I need encouragement, support, and love too?" But I don't shout. I know that I have Your love and support, so I lean on You. I withdraw to my room and have a good cry, and I trust that You are with me.

Jesus, I can't do it all by myself. Everything is falling apart around me. I'm having trouble holding it together, and I need You. My hope is in You. I know that You're with me, but I need to feel You. I want You to wrap me up warmly in Your love. I want You to fill me up with comfort and peace. Come, Lord Jesus. Take these burdens from me and give me rest.

"Come to me, all you who are weary and burdened, and I will give you rest."—Matthew 11:28

Attacking life with an "I can do it myself" attitude pushes Jesus away. Why? Because He wants you to depend on Him and not on yourself. When you feel overwhelmed, go to a quiet place and seek Him. Put Him in charge instead of you. When you give your burdens to Him, He will give you rest.

2

WE'RE IN THIS TOGETHER

Dear Jesus,

My house needs cleaning. There's laundry to do, and I'm always picking up someone's mess! It is an unending cycle. Some days it seems like all I do is clean.

I know that I need to calm down and take time to get organized, but life gets in my way. My calendar is full, and my to-do list is long. Just when I think I have things under control, something unexpected happens.

There's that word again, Lord—control. When will I learn that I cannot control every aspect of my life? You remind me of that so often, and yet I go my own way. I know, Lord: I need to clean away the clutter in my heart and make more room for You.

Jesus, I want You to be in control of my to-do list. Set my priorities. Show me what You want me to do. Remind me, please, that it is okay sometimes to say no, and help me get rid of any distractions that get in my way. Give me a cheerful heart as I tackle those things that need to get done.

I feel better now, Lord, because I know that we're in this together.

"Obey everything I have commanded you. And surely I am with you always, to the very end of the age."—Matthew 28:20

Ask Jesus to take charge of your day and to help you set your goals and priorities. Make Him a part of everything you do. If you begin to feel overwhelmed by a task, focus on Him. Remember that He is there beside you. You are not alone; the two of you work on your day together.

....

....

....

....

....

....

....

....

....

....

....

....

....

....

....

....

....

....

....

....

....

3
WORN OUT

Dear Jesus,

I feel overwhelmed. Every part of me is worn out. I'm physically, mentally, and spiritually tired. So please come, Lord Jesus. I need You.

I'm weary and I need rest. My body aches from all the stress that is lying on top of me and pressing me down. My mind overflows with worry. I ask myself, "What if?" and I imagine, "If only." Scenes from the past play through my head in rapid succession. I wonder, Was there more that I could have done? Did I do the right things?

Lord Jesus, my prayers have dwindled to almost nothing. All my words and begging You for answers have simply become, "Jesus, I need You." You seem so far away; still I hold tight, by faith, that You haven't abandoned me. You are a good and loving Shepherd, and I know that you won't leave me alone.

Come, Lord Jesus. Bring me rest. Please hurry. I need You.

My soul is weary with sorrow; strengthen me according to your word. Keep me from deceitful ways; be gracious to me and teach me your law. —Psalm 119:28–29

When your burden is too heavy, Jesus is there to take it. When you are too weary to walk, He carries you. If your prayer is nothing more than "Help," He hears you. You might feel that Jesus is lost in all the "junk" that fills up your head, but He will never leave you. He dwells in your heart. He loves you, and He will help you.

....

....

....

....

....

....

....

....

....

....

....

....

....

....

....

....

....

....

4
WEARY TRAVELER

Dear Jesus,

What is this journey I am on? The road has been long, and You know the obstacles I've met along the way. My path twists and turns. Sometimes it doubles back and sends me going in circles. How long, dear Jesus, before I reach my destination, that secret goal that You have planned for me?

Where am I going, Lord? Just when I think I know, You surprise me with a fork in the road. You send me in a new direction, one that I hadn't expected. Sometimes I just want to stop for a while. But You know me so well. You know that if I stop now, I might never continue on.

All along the way, You have been with me. You've listened to my prayers. You know what I want, and You know even better what I need. I trust You, Jesus, but are we almost there? I am weighed down and weary, and I need rest.

Commit your way to the LORD; trust in him and he will do this: he will make your righteous reward shine like the dawn. —Psalm 37:5-6

Maybe you have experienced a job loss or some other unexpected event that sent you hurtling toward the unknown. You might be on an uncertain path toward a new destination, and only God knows where you are headed. When moving on overwhelms you, remember to trust in the Lord. Rest in Him and allow Him to lead you. He knows where you are headed, and it is somewhere good.

....

....

....

....

....

....

....

....

....

....

....

....

....

....

....

....

5

TOO MUCH!

Dear Jesus,

When I look at everything I need to do, it's all just too much for me. Often it's so much that I just sit and do nothing. I can't get started because I don't know where to begin. It's such a problem for me, Lord, because while I'm overwhelmed and doing nothing, the pile grows bigger and bigger. Please help me.

First, I need strength just to dig in and get going. I need You to help me focus on one task at a time and turn my eyes from this mountain of stuff. I need strength to zero in on one thing at a time and keep going one small step at a time.

And, Jesus, I need help with giving myself credit for the tasks that I accomplish instead of scolding myself because I didn't get it all done. Help me, please, to set small goals. Then celebrate with me when I attain them.

I know that we can get this done together, Lord, if I keep my eyes steady on You instead of on the mountain.

The Lord makes firm the steps of the one who delights in him. —Psalm 37:23

Has your mountain of "stuff" grown so big that it seems impossible to knock it down? Then call on Jesus. Think about His ministry here on earth. He kept moving, one step at a time, one village at a time, often helping one person at a time. While He had the ability to accomplish everything all at once, He didn't. He worked steadily, task by task, need by need. Follow His example—be strong and dig in!

6

SING A NEW SONG

Dear Jesus,

My spouse tells me that all I ever do is complain. And he's right. Lord, You have opened my eyes and helped me look deep into my heart. I confess that I am a chronic complainer.

I complain whenever I have too much to do at work and around the house. I complain that I don't have enough help, and I complain that there aren't enough hours in my day. I allow everyday tasks to weigh me down, and then I complain to whoever will listen—and most often I complain to You.

"Oh, Jesus," I say, "I'm too busy. I need my family to help me more. I need You to take this stress away from me at work. I need more time for me. I need my spouse to be more understanding." There is some truth to all that, but what I really need is to change my attitude. When I praise You instead of complaining to You, I feel the burden lift. Help me, dear Jesus. I need my attitude readjusted.

Sing to the LORD a new song; sing to the LORD, all the earth. Sing to the LORD, praise his name.—Psalm 96:1-2

Do you often catch yourself complaining? You are not alone. In today's fast-paced world, it is easy to complain. But when complaining becomes chronic, it is time for an attitude adjustment. Along with bringing your burdens to the Lord, give Him generous praise. Throughout your day when you feel like complaining, praise Him. Practice doing this, and before long you will feel the burdens lift.

....

....

....

....

....

....

....

....

....

....

....

....

....

....

....

....

....

7

GOOD NEWS, BAD NEWS

Dear Jesus,

We need some good news! It seems lately that every newscast begins with news about a crime or a tragedy. Front-page newspaper stories almost always feature bad news. There's bad news everywhere, and it overwhelms me. Where has all the good news gone?

This world is Yours, and You are in it everywhere. Still, we rarely hear about You. In fact, there are those who try their hardest to keep You out of the world. With so many good people following Your example and doing good things, one would think that at least some of those positive things are newsworthy. But if the world hears about them at all, they are usually tucked away at the end of a newscast, taking a backseat to evil.

Dear Jesus, I know in my heart that You can turn this around. Take the attention from this overwhelming glut of bad news and turn the world's eyes toward You.

Finally, brothers and sisters, whatever is true, whatever is noble, whatever is right, whatever is pure, whatever is lovely, whatever is admirable—if anything is excellent or praiseworthy—think about such things.—Philippians 4:8

It does seem that bad news most often outweighs good news. Almost every day there are reports of crimes and sad events. But that doesn't have to overwhelm you! Dig a little deeper for the good news, and dwell on that instead of the bad. And remember that the best news is the good news that Jesus Christ came to save the world. In the end, He will overcome evil—forever.

8

OVERWHELMED WITH CHILDREN

Dear Jesus,

I'm tired. Each morning I rush to get myself ready before the kids are awake. After that, I rush to get them ready for their day. When breakfast is done, I rush to clean up the mess before I rush the kids to day care and school. Then I rush myself to work, where I rush some more before rushing back home just to rush again! Can you tell, Jesus, that I feel overwhelmed?

How did my life get so busy? I used to enjoy a long, hot bath. Now I am happy if I get a quick shower. At breakfast, I liked reading the newspaper and sipping coffee. Now I clean up spilled cereal and listen to little ones squabbling. At day's end my children need baths and cajoling to bedtime with the promise of one more story, but all I can think about is sleep and how little of it I get.

Jesus, I need You. Please calm me down. I know that children are a blessing, but I feel like instead of living life and enjoying it, I am only just surviving.

"But seek first his kingdom and his righteousness, and all these things will be given to you as well."—Matthew 6:33

Few things are more exhausting than parenthood, and Jesus understands. Whenever you feel emotionally or physically drained, it means that you need some quiet time alone with the Lord. Regardless of how busy you are, make Him your priority. He is able to calm you and give you the strength and stamina you need to raise your kids *and* enjoy living.

....

....

....

....

....

....

....

....

....

....

....

....

....

....

....

....

....

9

TURN IT AROUND

Dear Jesus,

You've taught me something. When I feel pressed down by some situation, I have the choice, and the ability, to turn things around.

When I am weighed down by constant negative comments, I can respond positively: "It's so beastly hot and humid out today." "Yes, but look at that beautiful, blue sky!" If my workload is too heavy, I don't have to be afraid to admit it. I can ask for help. And if someone wants me to do "one more thing" when I already have too much to do, I can choose to say no.

Why did it take me so long to learn this? You are my example, Jesus. You didn't try to do everything all by yourself. You had helpers and You still do today. You always turn the negative into something positive. When I put my faith in You and allow You to direct my steps, then I can do that too.

I feel so much lighter when I remember to turn things around. Thank You, Jesus, for a lesson well learned.

I have considered my ways and have turned my steps to your statutes. —Psalm 119:59

When you feel overwhelmed by negativity or have too much to do, remember that you can turn it around! The first thing Jesus did in His ministry was to enlist disciples to help Him. Who can *you* ask for help? Jesus also changed negative attitudes to positive, sometimes by what He said and sometimes by what He did. Put His example into practice in your own life. What can you do to turn things around?

....

....

....

....

....

....

....

....

....

....

....

....

....

....

....

....

....

10
OVERWHELMING JOY!

Dear Jesus,

The word overwhelmed *means to be inundated with too much of something. Usually it means something negative. But oh, how wonderful it is, Lord, to be overwhelmed by You and Your blessings and love.*

Every day You bless me in so many little ways, and when those big blessings come along I am indeed overwhelmed. You bless me beyond my expectations. A great, and yet humble, feeling comes with experiencing Your generous grace. How wonderful it is when you overwhelm me with Your endless mercy.

With overwhelming strength and power, You protect me from all evil. Your comforting presence overwhelms me when life presses down hard. I am overwhelmed by Your constant faithfulness and gentleness, and by Your ability to make all things good.

When I think of You suffering and dying for my sins, I am overwhelmed by both sadness and joy—You died so that I might live with You forever. What an amazing gift!

Jesus, it feels so good to be overwhelmed by You. Please overwhelm me some more!

We have all received one blessing after another.
God's grace is not limited.—John 1:16 NIRV

Just knowing Jesus and experiencing His mercy, grace, and love should overwhelm you! Think of all the blessings He showers on you every day: little blessings, like your child's hugs and kisses, and big blessings, like solving your problems or healing a broken relationship. Open your heart up all the way to Jesus, and ask Him to overwhelm you with goodness. Then, with gratefulness, bask in overwhelming joy.

REFLECTIONS ON
FEELING OVERWHELMED

REFLECTIONS ON
FEELING OVERWHELMED

....

....

....

....

....

....

....

....

....

....

....

....

....

....

....

....

....

....

....

....

JESUS,
I NEED
YOU . . .

WHEN I FEEL GRATITUDE

1

YOU BRING OUT THE BEST IN ME

Dear Jesus,

You bring out the best in me. When I am compassionate, kind, caring, or selfless, it is because I have learned by Your example. When I work to serve others, it is You working through me. You make me want to work harder and better because I want others to see You in me.

Jesus, You bring out the best in me. Every day You open my eyes to so many little things that fill my heart with joy: a child's laugh, a friendly smile, the sunrise, the soft sound of gentle rain. Because You calm my storms, I am able to provide comfort to others. You give me strength when I am weak and courage when I am afraid. You forgive me, and by Your example, I am able to forgive others. Best of all, Jesus, You are always right. You help me make right decisions.

I can't imagine how hollow my life would be without You. When I put my trust in You, I know that whatever happens, You are with me. You are my Savior, my partner, and my best friend. I love You.

Even more, I consider everything to be nothing compared to knowing Christ Jesus my Lord. To know him is the best thing of all. —Philippians 3:8 NIRV

Jesus brings out the best in you when you make Him your everything. If you trust Him with every part of your life, your attitude shifts from negative to positive. You worry less as you shift your focus from what's wrong to what's right. The more you try to be like Jesus, the more you will feel His presence in your heart.

....

....

....

....

....

....

....

....

....

....

....

....

....

....

....

....

....

....

2

WHAT A BEAUTIFUL DAY!

Dear Jesus,

Today is such a lovely day. In the distance, snowcapped mountains reach for the clearest blue sky, and the sun's reflection has turned the lake into a sea of diamonds. The scent of pine drifts through the woods, and birds' sweet songs fill the air. Right here, right now, the world seems so perfect. Lord, oh, how wonderful that Your perfection shines through in an imperfect world!

A doe rests in a clearing with her fawn. Squirrels and chipmunks rustle through leaves on the forest floor, and yet I can hear myself breathe. The sounds of silence are everywhere in this perfect place because You are all around me.

Jesus, if this isn't perfection, I can only imagine the garden of Eden. How wonderful it must have been: the sights, sounds, and scents, all of them flawless, every need met.

I stand here taking in all of Your creation, and You remind me that an even more beautiful place is awaiting me in heaven, a place with a sky more perfect than this sky, warmth more perfect than the warmth of this sun, sounds sweeter than the birds' songs.

Oh, Jesus! I am so blessed.

> "See, I am doing a new thing! Now it springs up; do you not perceive it? I am making a way in the wilderness and streams in the wasteland."—Isaiah 43:19

The eighteenth-century poet Minnie Aumonier wrote, "There is always music amongst the trees in the garden, but our hearts must be very quiet to hear it." God's amazing creation is all around you. Do you see it? Quiet your heart and soak up all the beauty that surrounds you today. Give thanks for God's perfection in an imperfect world.

3

THANK YOU FOR JOY

Dear Jesus,

Sometimes I crave that unbridled joy that comes with childhood. I think of how it felt to pedal my bike fast, the wind whipping though my hair, without a care in the world. I long for the innocence to see life through a child's rose-colored glasses, to laugh, sing, and play again.

With each passing year, joy has been pushed deeper down inside me. But, Jesus, You remind me that the child who I was still exists in my heart. You open my eyes to joy all around me. You show me that joy is more than happiness. It is contentment knowing that You are with me. It is in Your creation, in the beauty of the earth. It is in a smile, a kind word, a laugh, and a song. But, most of all, joy comes with worship and thankfulness for You.

Yes, happiness is temporary, but joy is eternal. It exists regardless of my circumstances. It is about finding joyful innocence in my grown-up heart. It is accepting Your love with a simple, childlike faith. Joy is in discovering new things about You every day. Oh, thank You, dear Jesus, for joy!

> The precepts of the LORD are right, giving joy
> to the heart. The commands of the LORD are
> radiant, giving light to the eyes. —Psalm 19:8

Anne Frank wrote in her diary, "I don't think about all the misery, but about the beauty that still remains."4 If anyone had reason not to be joyful, it was Anne. But she knew that joy was more than happiness; it existed in spite of her circumstances. You can experience that kind of joy too. Today, ask Jesus to show you the true meaning of joy.

....

....

....

....

....

....

....

....

....

....

....

....

....

....

....

....

4

WHEN I GRUMBLE

Dear Jesus,

I complain sometimes. I guess I'm no different from anyone else—we all complain. But I would like to complain less often.

In the summertime when it is hot, I complain that it is too hot. In the winter, I complain that it is too cold. I complain when there is too much snow, not enough rain, or when the wind blows too hard. When my children don't behave, I complain. I grumble when I have too much to do, when something or someone spoils my plans, and when I face a difficult task. Jesus, I confess I even whine sometimes when I don't get my way.

I'm sorry for when I complain. I know that it disrespects You, and You give me Your best all the time. My goal, Lord, is to stand out in a positive way in a world of complainers. I want to be mindful of what Paul says in the Bible: "Be thankful in all circumstances."

Help me, Jesus, to be aware of those times when I grumble and complain. Whisper in my heart that there is a better way. Remind me that in all things I need to have an attitude of gratitude.

Do everything without grumbling or arguing.—Philippians 2:14

Wouldn't it be wonderful if we could be perfect like Jesus and never complain? But we are not perfect, and all of us complain sometimes. When you find yourself complaining, confess it to Jesus and ask for His forgiveness. Ask Him to change your complaints to words of gratitude and praise.

....

....

....

....

....

....

....

....

....

....

....

....

....

....

....

....

....

....

....

5

YOU LIFT ME UP

Dear Jesus,

How awesome You are! You lift me high above my circumstances. You can take a day that begins badly and turn it completely around. It might come through something shiny and bright or something ordinary and small, but You always find ways to light up my days.

Jesus, You lift me up with Your perfect timing. When I need help, You send it to me in the form of a human helper or by sharing with me Your knowledge and Your strength. When I need a respite from my work, You lift me up with enjoyable little diversions. When life gets me down, You find ways to make me smile. You help me rise above the bad news of the day by balancing it with the good news from Your Word. You raise me up above my human imperfections and make me perfect in You.

Oh, Jesus, You are so awesome! I'm grateful that You care so much about me. Your arms are strong enough to lift me above any barrier that life puts in my way. Thank You so much for brightening my days.

> He lifted me out of the slimy pit, out of the
> mud and mire; he set my feet on a rock and
> gave me a firm place to stand. —Psalm 40:2

Certainly, if Jesus made the blind see and the lame walk upright and strong, He can turn your life around for the better. He has the same great power now as when He lived on earth in a human body. Whenever you need to rise above your circumstances, call on Him, and He will lift you up.

6

THANK YOU FOR LAUGHTER

Dear Jesus,

Thank You for making me laugh today. You opened my eyes and my ears to many funny little things.

I enjoyed hearing my children's silly jokes and riddles. Even when the punch lines are nonsense, the way my kids find delight in telling their jokes makes me laugh. I laughed when I watched my husband playing with our children, when he used those ridiculous voices with them and made them giggle. I love it when our family plays and laughs together. Thank you for creating those experiences for us.

I laughed with my friends today too. We had one of those preplanned girl get-togethers where we shared our life stories and giggled. Thank you, Jesus, that we can laugh at our circumstances and at ourselves.

You even opened my eyes to amusing things in Your creation: a lanky, gray squirrel hanging by its toes, stretching to steal seed from a feeder, a mother duck stopping traffic to walk her ducklings across a busy street. I must remember to look more often and watch more closely for the humorous sights You put in front of me.

What a great day it has been! Thank You, Jesus, for laughter.

He will fill your mouth with laughter. Shouts of joy will come from your lips.—Job 8:21 NIRV

The great Martin Luther offered this humorous quote: "If you're not allowed to laugh in heaven, I don't want to go there."[5] Surely God provides laughter for us in heaven just as He does here on earth. Laughter is a part of His creation. So lighten up a little today. Allow yourself to laugh!

....

....

....

....

....

....

....

....

....

....

....

....

....

....

....

....

....

....

DEAR JESUS, I LOVE YOU

Dear Jesus,

I love You. Your presence is like a cool breeze on a hot summer night. When I am tired and weary, You refresh me. When words sting, You heal my hurt. Jesus, the sweetness of Your voice calms me when I am afraid, and it comforts me when I mourn. You lift me above the world's dissonance and give me peace.

Whether I am in a crowd of unfamiliar people or in the company of my loved ones, You are there. I never worry about being alone, because You are always with me. You find me when I am lost, save me from the enemy's traps, and rescue me when I am in danger. No problem is too great for you to solve.

Oh, how wonderful You are! Powerful, yet gentle; sweet, but strong; wise and willing. You sit on a throne at the right hand of God, and as great as You are, You love me. I can't believe how much You love me. And Jesus—I love You too!

> *I love those who love me, and those who seek me find me.—Proverbs 8:17*

It is through our relationship with Jesus that we have eternal life. He loves us so much that He sacrificed His own life so that we can be washed clean of sin. Every minute Jesus is with us, loving us. Turn your thoughts toward Him today. Meditate on all that He does for you. Give thanks and, most of all, tell Him that you love Him.

8

THE LITTLE THINGS

Dear Jesus,

Thank You for the little things You do that I take for granted, things like waking me in the morning and setting a new day before me, bright, fresh, and filled with hope and expectation. In the morning, You awaken my senses. You open my ears to the birds' sweet singing mingled with the gentle stirring of my children waking. You send the comforting scent of coffee drifting up the stairs, inviting me to breakfast.

All day long, You surprise me with unexpected gifts of laughter, kindness, fellowship, and encouragement. When I run out of patience, You give me more, and when I run out of time, You set my priorities. You support me through moments of frustration and forgive me when I lose my temper. If I lack understanding, You provide knowledge. If I think I know everything, You remind me to be humble.

At day's end when I'm weary, Jesus, You grant me rest. When You send me off to sleep, I know that You will give me protection through the night. You refresh me and make me ready for another new day.

I'm grateful, Jesus, for all the little things.

> *Sing and make music from your heart to the Lord, always giving thanks to God the Father for everything, in the name of our Lord Jesus Christ.* —Ephesians 5:19–20

Each breath you take, every beat of your heart, is a God-given gift. He is the root of your existence; He created you. Every minute of your life, Jesus is with you. He wakes you, guides you through your day, and tucks you into bed at night. Then He stays at your side while you sleep. Today, and every day, thank Him for all the little things He does for you.

....

....

....

....

....

....

....

....

....

....

....

....

....

....

....

....

....

....

9

BEAUTIFUL CREATION

Dear Jesus,

Thank You for showing me that I need to open my eyes and soak up earth's beauty. Your Creation is perfect and pure, a flawless work of art, majestic in every way. The deepest valleys and the highest mountains reflect Your greatness. Lord, the world, and everything in it, is Your masterpiece. If I forgot to look, I would miss so much.

Creations by famous painters, sculptors, and photographers fill the greatest museums in the world. Visitors admire the artists' unique uses of shape, form, and color. The works of Van Gogh, Picasso, Cézanne—priceless.

But they are nothing when compared with the works of Your hands. None of the great creative masters could hang the moon and the stars or form great oceans out of nothing. They might paint images in dazzling daybreak colors, but none could set the sun on fire and send the earth spinning round.

You are the one who is beautiful beyond words, and everything You make mirrors Your beauty. Thank You, dear Jesus, for opening my eyes.

In the beginning, the Word was already there. The Word was with God, and the Word was God. He was with God in the beginning. All things were made through him.—John 1:1–3 NIRV

We are so much at home here on earth that we forget what a spectacular creation earth is. Tell God thank You for being the greatest Creator of all. Everything made by Him is perfect—day and night, changing seasons, the cycles of life. Take time. Open your eyes and meditate on the beauty around you.

....

....

....

....

....

....

....

....

....

....

....

....

....

....

....

....

....

....

....

10

THOSE WHO SERVE

Dear Jesus,

Thank You for the caring hearts of those who serve. You send them, the strong and faithful, to do Your good works. Like angels, they exist all around us, often unnoticed until we need them.

Law enforcement officers risk their lives to keep us peaceful and safe. Firefighters put the lives of others before their own to save us from smoke and flames. Soldiers volunteer to fight for our freedoms and protect us from evil. Doctors and nurses help heal the sick, chaplains provide comfort to those who hurt, teachers teach, ministers preach, missionaries travel the world sharing Your message with those who have not heard—disciples, each and every one!

Protect them, dear Lord, those who put others before themselves. Bless them as they go about Your work. Give them the physical and emotional strength that they need for their jobs. Guide their decisions and their steps, and especially, put it in our hearts to remember to thank them.

> *Sitting down, Jesus called the Twelve and said,*
> *"Anyone who wants to be first must be the*
> *very last, and the servant of all."—Mark 9:35*

Do you remember to thank God for them—the crossing guard at your child's school, the police officer directing traffic at a busy intersection where the stoplight isn't working, the teenage neighbor girl who came right over to babysit when you had to run an unexpected errand? Jesus' helpers are all around you, meeting your everyday needs. Notice what they do, and remember to tell them thank you!

....

....

....

....

....

....

....

....

....

....

....

....

....

....

....

....

....

REFLECTIONS ON GRATITUDE

....

....

....

....

....

....

....

....

....

....

....

....

....

....

....

....

....

....

....

....

REFLECTIONS ON GRATITUDE

JESUS, I NEED YOU . . .

WHEN I FEEL HEARTACHE

1

LET GO OF THE PAIN

Dear Jesus,

I definitely feel like I'm living in the past today. Old memories of not-so-good times swirl around inside me, remnants of an old storm. Lord, I'm dwelling on things again, things I should have left behind. Why is it so hard to let go? I have forgiven past transgressions, but I haven't forgotten. Perhaps I never will. The past remains a part of me.

You have forgiven my sins, and You want me to forgive the sins of others. I think I have done that. But the pain remains in my memories. I still hurt.

Help me, Jesus, to let go. Instead of being consumed by a hurtful past, I want to focus on a bright future. You have promised me abundant life here on earth and an eternal future with You in heaven. What more could I ask for?

Today, I will turn my thoughts toward You and what lies ahead. Every day, whenever the past haunts me, I will try to remember that You have plans for me, and all of them are good. Jesus, open the door to my future today. Hold my hand. Let's go there together.

Brothers and sisters, I do not consider myself yet to have taken hold of it. But one thing I do: Forgetting what is behind and straining toward what is ahead.—Philippians 3:13

Yesterday's pain serves only to dim Christ's light in the present. Allow His light to shine brightly in your heart by giving past hurts to Him. Jesus is the one who can make it all better. He wants to heal your wounds and set you on the path to an abundant future.

FITTING IN

Dear Jesus,

I feel cut off from the world. Everyone seems to fit like a piece in a puzzle while I'm just a square peg in a round hole. I don't fit into the tight alliance that most groups of friends have. I am a drifter, a thinker, and my thoughts are different from theirs. I guess You might say that they don't "get" me.

Jesus, if it weren't for You, I think I would feel lonely. Even in a crowd of friends, I sometimes feel isolated. I am so grateful that You are always with me in my heart, guiding me and loving me. Friends have left me, but You never have and You never will. You get me. You understand my thoughts, and You give me plenty to think about.

Maybe, Jesus, You could help me find some like-minded friends to hang out with. You must know exactly where I fit.

The LORD God said, "It is not good for
the man to be alone. I will make a helper
suitable for him."—Genesis 2:18

Maybe there are times when you feel that you don't fit in. Feeling uncomfortable with the company you keep can lead to loneliness, and Jesus does not want you to be alone. He is always with you. But it is not good to go through life without like-minded friends. If you need a better fit, ask Jesus to help you. He knows where you belong and He will lead you there.

....

....

....

....

....

....

....

....

....

....

....

....

....

....

....

....

3
LOSING A LOVED ONE

Dear Jesus,

Someone I love has died, and my heart is broken. I want to be strong, knowing that this person is free from suffering. They are with You in heaven now, well and strong. But still my heart aches.

By faith, I know that I will see my loved one again. But having them out of my sight makes me sad. I long to see them, to hug them once more, and to hear their voice.

In my sadness, I've asked You why. Why did my loved one have to suffer? Why did death come too soon? I know that Your answers are beyond my understanding now, but maybe someday when we meet face-to-face you will share them with me.

Jesus, when Your friend Lazarus died, You wept. Now I weep for my loved one. Surely You understand my pain. So please, Jesus, comfort me. Take the ache in my heart and ease it with Your gentle, sweet love. Wrap me up warmly in Your embrace until I am healed.

Where, O death, is your victory? Where, O death, is your sting?—1 Corinthians 15:55

Jesus understands loss and heartache. After all, He is God, and when we chose sin over Him, oh, how it hurt Him! And He was brokenhearted on the cross when He felt that His Father had abandoned Him. Everyone suffers heartache when they lose someone they love. But there is comfort in knowing the Lord. Ask Him to comfort you, and He will. Jesus understands and He loves you.

4

LOVES ME, LOVES ME NOT

Dear Jesus,

We were so much in love. We stood before our family and friends, all those years ago, and pledged our love to each other and also to You. We promised to stay together forever. No matter what. Always! But now he says that he's fallen out of love with me. He's moving on with somebody else. Oh, Jesus! It hurts so bad.

I feel not good enough, like some old piece of junk that has lost its usefulness. Thrown away. Replaced by a shiny, new model. In my heart, I know that I'm not useless, nor am I junk. You made me, after all, so I can't be garbage. But still, I feel that way.

I need You so much right now. Please, Jesus, be all those things to me that my husband is not. I know that You love me just as I am, and I know that You will help me through this. Just be gentle with me, Lord. I need Your tender and healing touch, because right now I'm bruised and broken.

The LORD is my rock and my fort. He is the One who saves me. My God is my rock. I go to him for safety. He is like a shield to me. He's the power that saves me. He's my place of safety. —Psalm 18:2 NIRV

For most, a separation or divorce brings enormous pain. What once appeared so certain is shattered into pieces, none of which seem to fit together anymore. In this situation what can you do? Lean hard into Jesus and allow Him to help you. He will never throw you away or treat you like junk. He made you and He loves you. Trust that, although the pain seems unbearable, Jesus will bring you through it.

....

....

....

....

....

....

....

....

....

....

....

....

....

....

....

....

....

5

PARENTHOOD PAIN

Dear Jesus,

Being the parent of a teen comes with a roller coaster of emotions. I love my child with all my heart, but sometimes he makes me so angry. His poor choices have hurt me, but what hurts even more is the way that he treats me. He was not raised to be disrespectful, but he is. He barely speaks to me anymore. The pain that I feel is so deep.

Dear Jesus, my child needs You. He is like the lost sheep in the parable. He has left You and gone his way. The kids he hangs out with I disapprove of, and their influence on him is strong. Please find my child and bring him back to me.

And, Jesus, I need You too. Parenting an older teen is one of the hardest things I have ever done, and also one of the most hurtful. Will you please replace the pain I feel with Your strength and guidance? Together, let's save my son.

"Suppose one of you has a hundred sheep and loses one of them. Doesn't he leave the ninety-nine in the open country and go after the lost sheep until he finds it? And when he finds it, he joyfully puts it on his shoulders and goes home."—Luke 15:4–6

Parenting a child through the years from teen to adult is indeed a challenge. Maybe you have found yourself in this situation. If your child goes off course and you are unable to redirect him, remember that you can always count on Jesus for help. Prayer is important, and so is action. Ask Jesus to make it clear to you what you can do to bring your child home.

....

....

....

....

....

....

....

....

....

....

....

....

....

....

....

....

....

6

WORDS *CAN* HURT ME

Dear Jesus,

I confess to You that I have gossiped. I have said things about others that I would never say in their presence. And, Jesus, when I did it, I never gave it a second thought. But now, gossip is the only thing on my mind, because I am a victim of it.

Lord, I am learning that shameful words wound deeply. Like arrows, they pierce the heart and tear into the soul. Unkind words especially hurt when delivered by a loved one. They sting, shattering trust into a million tiny pieces.

How can I be angry with the one who hurt me when I have hurt others in the same way? My pain is veiled in guilty feelings. I am in need of healing as well as forgiveness.

Jesus, I have learned a lesson in this heartache. And with Your help, I will watch the words that come from my lips so that they will never again cause anyone to hurt.

The words of the reckless pierce like swords, but the tongue of the wise brings healing. —Proverbs 12:18

Are you guilty of gossip? Have words ever hurt you? The pain caused by reckless words can hurt deeper and longer than physical pain. Words stay with us, they stick hard, and unlike body aches that can be eased with medication, the only cure for hurtful words is forgiveness. Think about what you say, and speak in ways that will please the Lord.

....

....

....

....

....

....

....

....

....

....

....

....

....

....

....

....

....

....

7

A NEW CALLING

Dear Jesus,

My life has been filled with heartache. I don't have to tell You that; You already know. You and I have shared many long nights discussing the reasons why, and from our conversations I have learned that why doesn't matter. What does matter is how I react when faced with emotional pain. What matters most is my relationship with You.

Jesus, through years of heartache You have molded my spirit. You have refined and tempered me, made me strong. Your mercy brought softness into my hard space and caused me to look outside of myself toward others. You opened my eyes to the pain all around me and reminded me that I am not alone in my suffering.

Now, Jesus, I think I am receiving Your answer to my endless asking, "Why?" You have put it in my heart to help others who are suffering from their own heartaches. I can do that now with empathy. I can lend understanding and aid. Jesus, put me to work. What can I do to help them?

My brothers and sisters, you will face all kinds of trouble. When you do, think of it as pure joy. Your faith will be put to the test. You know that when that happens it will produce in you the strength to continue. The strength to keep going must be allowed to finish its work. Then you will be all you should be. You will have everything you need. —James 1:2–4 NIRV

Not only can Jesus ease your pain, but sometimes He uses it to lead you to a new calling. Ask most volunteers, and they will tell you that they experienced a heartache that led them to serve others. Just as Romans 8:28 says, "And we know that all things work together for good to them that love God, to them who are the called according to his purpose" (KJV).

8

JESUS, DO YOU WEEP?

Dear Jesus,

Do You weep when You see what we've done? Does it break Your heart? Our earth, this place that God the Father created in flawless, peaceful beauty, has become swathed in sin. It's sad—so very sad. And no one is to blame but mankind.

I wonder sometimes why people continue to make such poor choices. You give us all the freedom to choose. We can choose to follow You and make the world a better place, or we can choose sin. Why do we continuously choose sin when it only leads to heartache?

I am grateful, Lord, that You haven't given up on us. You suffered such pain and anguish on the cross so that those who love You will have eternal life. You continue to love us in spite of our sinful imperfection, and still we cause You pain.

Jesus, You are the world's hero, the one who brings peace in the midst of this earthly storm, and we need You. When sin makes You sad, Lord, remember those who love You. We weep along with You.

Again and again they put God to the test. They made the Holy One of Israel sad and angry.—Psalm 78:41 NIRV

We read in Genesis 6:6, "The LORD was very sad that he had made man on the earth. His heart was filled with pain" (NIRV). Have you thought that God experiences heartache too? We know that Jesus wept. The Bible tells us so. When you pray about your own heartache, or someone else's, consider also the pain that Jesus feels over the world's sin. Then say a prayer and tell Him that you love Him.

....

....

....

....

....

....

....

....

....

....

....

....

....

....

....

....

9
NOT GOOD ENOUGH

Dear Jesus,

Whatever I do, it is never good enough. I feel that way both at work and at home. Some days I am so depressed that I can barely get out of bed in the morning to face another day.

I try my best to be a good worker, wife, and mom, but it isn't enough. What does it take, Lord, to please people? What will make them happy? I'm willing to do whatever You tell me to do, because I don't know how much more of this I can take.

I don't feel good about myself at all. I used to think of myself as being bright and talented. If I set a goal, I usually achieved it, and then I pushed myself to accomplish something bigger. I had confidence in my ability, and I always knew where I was headed. But now, Jesus, I'm sad all the time, and I feel like a loser.

I know that You love me and will help me. Please restore me and take this sadness away. I need You!

The Spirit of God has made me; the breath of the Almighty gives me life. —Job 33:4

Depression often happens when you expect too much of yourself or when you put too much emphasis on pleasing others. If your self-esteem tumbles and you feel depressed, remember that God made you in His image. He is not a loser, nor are you. Your goal is to please God. You accomplish that by listening to Him and doing your best. Don't let the world convince you that you aren't good enough—because you are!

10

NOTHING CAN HARM ME

Dear Jesus,

I believe that whatever happens, You will lift me high above the pain. Nothing can harm me, because I have You.

When the storm rushes at me fast, when the flood threatens me—water rising, swirling hard—You save me. You set my feet on the high ground and You shelter me safely beneath Your wings. When lightning flashes and thunder booms loudly, You take away my fears.

The road is long, Lord, but when I grow weary, You carry me. You never leave my side. We're on this journey together, You and I, and I know You will not fail me. When the pain overtakes me, You dry my tears. You give me courage to not give up. Always, You are the source of my strength.

You know where and how this journey will end, and You remind me that the sadness and pain is not forever. Dear Jesus, I could not do this without You. I love You so much!

He heals the brokenhearted and binds up their wounds.—Psalm 147:3

In "The Ballad of Reading Gaol," Oscar Wilde wrote, "How else but through a broken heart / May Lord Christ enter in?"[6] When heartbreak comes, throw open the door to your heart and welcome Jesus in. He is the one who will not only begin your healing process but also see it through to the end. Trust Him. He loves you, and He wants to help.

....
....
....
....
....
....
....
....
....
....
....
....
....
....
....
....
....
....

REFLECTIONS ON HEARTACHE

REFLECTIONS ON HEARTACHE

JESUS,
I NEED
YOUR . . .

COMFORT

1

YOU ARE MY REFUGE

Dear Jesus,

Thank You for providing security in an insecure world. You warned, "Nation will rise against nation, and kingdom against kingdom. There will be earthquakes in various places, and famines. These are the beginning of birth pains" (Mark 13:8). All of this and more will signal Your coming. But You also said, "Do not be alarmed" (Mark 13:7). Jesus, when things spiral downward, You are my refuge, my soft place to fall.

In this ever-changing world, You never change. Every promise You have made will be fulfilled. Whatever happens, no matter how disturbing, Your love will see me through. Because You love me, I will not be afraid.

Jesus, when the world seems dark, You give Your people light. When the valleys are deep, You lift them high onto the mountaintop. You are strength in weakness and hope in despair. Your precepts never change, nor does Your purpose. You are always holy, always just, and always right. Most of all, You are there for us, a Father protecting His children. Nothing can harm me as long as I put my faith in You. I am safe in Your presence, Lord. Thank You so much for Your love.

> "Do not fear, for I have redeemed
> you; I have summoned you by name;
> you are mine."—Isaiah 43:1

Today's world can be a frightening place. Everywhere you look, there seems to be bad news. But as a Christian you have the gift of looking beyond what's negative and seeing Jesus. When you view the world through Him, there is no fear. He is your refuge and your strength. Put all of your trust in Him, and He will protect you.

2
WATCH OVER MY CHILDREN

Dear Jesus,

I come to You in prayer today asking that You watch over my children. Whenever they are out of my sight, I worry. I know, Lord, that You are with them all the time; but still, I worry.

Jesus, the world is such an unpredictable place, a dangerous place for children who often do unpredictable things. Please keep my children safe and help them remember what I have taught them. Watch over them especially when I can't, and also give wisdom and guidance to those whom I entrust with their care.

As my children grow and become more independent, continue to watch over them. Wrap Your arms around them, Jesus. Draw them close to You, and protect them from making wrong choices. Make them hungry for Your teaching, and fill them up with good judgment.

Thank You so much for giving them to me to nourish and love. Help me always be a good parent to them—the kind of parent that You are to me.

I love You, Jesus.

All your children will be taught by the LORD,
and great will be their peace.—Isaiah 54:13

Sometimes parents forget that they are children too—God's children. Surely if He watches over you, He watches over Your little ones too. When you find yourself worrying about your children, call on Jesus. He is with them, and you can trust Him.

3
JUST HANGING OUT

Dear Jesus,

I love it when we hang out together, just the two of us, You and me. You have the amazing ability to lead us to places where there are no distractions. Sometimes we enjoy a quiet walk together, or you meet me at the kitchen table for a cup of tea. Of course I can't see You, but I feel You all around me, and I hear Your voice in my heart. I get up early to meet You in the quiet of the morning, and often You are the last one whose voice I hear before I fall asleep at night.

The time I spend with You is precious, Jesus. It makes me feel so special knowing how much You love me. I'm honored that You want to be with me and help me through life. Whether it's to share in some small pleasure or to conquer a roadblock in my way, You meet me wherever I am. We go through life together, the best of friends.

Thank You, dear Jesus. Thank You for hanging out with me.

Come near to God and he will come near to you. —James 4:8

Jesus' voice is most clear when you spend quiet time alone with Him. This quiet time should be about relationship, not ritual. Be still with Jesus, read the Bible, meditate, and listen for His voice. Praise Him, talk to Him. Treat this intimate time as you would with a dear, trusted friend.

....

....

....

....

....

....

....

....

....

....

....

....

....

....

....

....

....

....

4

QUIET TIME

Dear Jesus,

Thank You for quiet times with my family. I love the calm bedtime ritual, reading to the children, answering their sleepy questions, and tucking them into bed. And I love those quiet conversations with my spouse after the kids are asleep: cuddling, watching a movie together, resting in our love—and Yours. A sense of peace surrounds me, a peace, I know, that comes from You.

Jesus, I'm grateful for those quiet times that I spend with You: praying, praising You, listening to You in my heart, meditating on Your Word. Those times are special. I feel closest to You then. Somehow You always manage to find a quiet place where we can meet and spend time together.

I think of David's words in the Twenty-third Psalm: "He leads me beside quiet waters, he refreshes my soul" (v. 2–3). That's what You do for me, Jesus. You refresh me in the quiet moments of my day. Thank You.

But I have calmed and quieted myself, I am like a weaned child with its mother; like a weaned child I am content.—Psalm 131:2

Jesus brings peace to families. He adds His gentleness and love to quiet times spent together. Do your best to build quiet time into your family's schedule, time spent with your children and spouse. Also, spend quiet time alone with Jesus. Rest in Him, and allow Him to refresh you.

....

....

....

....

....

....

....

....

....

....

....

....

....

....

....

....

....

....

....

....

5

JESUS ALL AROUND

Dear Jesus,

You are all around me. You are in each story with a happy ending, and if an ending isn't happy, You bring comfort to broken hearts. Jesus, I see You in hospitals, guiding doctors and nurses and comforting the sick and their families. You are in nursing homes, in meals served to the poor, and in shelter provided to the homeless. Wherever there is hope, Jesus, there You are.

I find You in my children's happy drawings and in their loving hugs and kisses. You exist in my husband's strength and faithfulness and in my ability to serve my family even when I am tired.

I hear You in the exuberant joy of Sunday morning choirs and in my pastor's well-chosen words. You are in every prayer and in every need met. Best of all, Jesus, You are with me in my heart and in my thoughts, every day and forever.

Shout aloud and sing for joy, people of Zion, for great is the Holy One of Israel among you. —Isaiah 12:6

In the busyness of your days, remember Jesus. If you look for Him, you will find Him all around you. He is in everything good and in every act of goodness. Take some time today to notice Jesus all around you. Look for Him in the most unlikely places— you might be surprised to find Him there.

....

....

....

....

....

....

....

....

....

....

....

....

....

....

....

....

....

....

....

6

GRANT ME PEACE

Dear Jesus,

You are the Prince of Peace, and I need peace today. Will You help me find it? You know the problem that I'm struggling with. It makes me feel anxious and my mind is filled with worry. My heart is empty and I don't know what to do. I hate being locked up with this storm that's inside me. Dear Jesus, I need You.

I remember what Paul said in Philippians 4:6–7: "Do not be anxious about anything, but in every situation, by prayer and petition, with thanksgiving, present your requests to God. And the peace of God, which transcends all understanding, will guard your hearts and your minds in Christ Jesus."

Paul's advice is straightforward and simple. If I leave my problem at Your feet today, and if I ask You to grant me peace, You will. By faith, I believe. I believe that if I keep my mind fixed on You, this anxious feeling will go away.

Come, Lord Jesus, guard my heart and my mind; give me peace.

"The Lord turn his face toward you and give you peace."—Numbers 6:26

Finding peace in Christ Jesus takes practice. It means learning to give all your cares to Him, resting in His love, and trusting that He will work things out. Giving up control is hard. It is something that you have to do again and again until it becomes a habit. When you learn to put all of your trust in Jesus, He will replace your anxiety with peace. Ask Him to help you. He is ready and willing.

....

....

....

....

....

....

....

....

....

....

....

....

....

....

....

7

COMFORT MY FRIEND

Dear Jesus,

There is a woman I work with who has just experienced a tragic loss. You know who she is and You know what happened. I come to You today asking that You help my friend.

I don't know what else to do for her but pray. She has pulled away from us—her coworkers and friends. When she has to be with us, she acts as if nothing has happened. If we offer condolences and help, she replies, "I'm fine." Jesus, I know that she is not fine. What happened has left her alone, without a family, and I want to help fill that gap. I want her to know that I, and many others, am there for her.

If I can't help, Jesus, I am sure that You can. You are with her during the darkest, loneliest times, and I know that You will never leave her alone. Open her heart to You so she can feel Your love. Comfort her and dry her tears. And, Jesus, if there is any way I can help, please show me how. I love my friend, and oh, how she needs You.

> When Jesus entered Capernaum, a Roman commander came to him. He asked Jesus for help. "Lord," he said, "my servant lies at home and can't move. He is suffering terribly." Jesus said, "I will go and heal him."—Matthew 8:5–7 NIRV

Some people have a difficult time accepting help from others. In the worst of times they may avoid their friends and pull deep inside themselves. Sometimes you might feel that there is little you can do to help. But there is something! You can bring that person before the Lord in prayer. Pray and keep praying for them. Then wait for Jesus to open the doors to meet your friend's needs.

....

....

....

....

....

....

....

....

....

....

....

....

....

....

....

....

8

WHEN I NEED REST

Dear Jesus,

I am grateful to You for teaching me the importance of rest.

When You lived on earth, sometimes You separated from Your disciples and the crowds and went to spend time alone with Your Father. You knew how to refresh and recharge Your body and soul so that You could go about Your work relaxed and ready. Yours is the example I follow whenever I feel weary.

When I am tired, Your words come to mind: "Come to me, all you who are weary and burdened, and I will give you rest" (Matthew 11:28). I look forward to going off alone with You to pray and read the Bible. I meditate on Your goodness, and then sometimes I lie down and allow myself to slip into sweet sleep, knowing that You are with me.

Thank You, Jesus, for being my place of refreshment and rest. Thank You for being a soft place of peace.

Then Jesus said to his apostles, "Come with me by yourselves to a quiet place. You need to get some rest."—Mark 6:31 NIRV

Rest is important. Jesus, as busy as He was, made time to rest. To rest means more than taking a nap or settling down with a good book. The Bible reminds us to "rest in the Lord" (Psalm 37:7 KJV). That means getting alone with Him to spend time in meditation and prayer. And when you do lie down to sleep, remember that He is with you when you are at rest and always.

9
WHEN I AM SICK

Dear Jesus,

I need You. My body is sick, and I am in pain. I can't sleep; my mind is so full of anxious thoughts. I need healing, and I need comfort.

Dear Jesus, I come to You empty-handed asking for Your mercy. I believe that You can heal me. Will You, Lord? I leave that up to You because You have a plan for me, and I know it is a perfect plan. Maybe you won't heal me on this side of heaven—but maybe You will! That is my hope.

Help me, Jesus, to remain faithful in the midst of this illness. I know that You are with me and watching over me night and day. I believe in Your love for me. I know that You will comfort me if I can keep my mind set on You instead of sickness and pain. Help me, Jesus! Fill me up with You. Comfort me with Your sweet love.

Praise be to the God and Father of our Lord Jesus Christ, the Father of compassion and the God of all comfort, who comforts us in all our troubles, so that we can comfort those in any trouble with the comfort we ourselves receive from God.—2 Corinthians 1:3–4

Illness is a true test of faith. Physical discomfort and anxious thoughts make it difficult to focus on Christ's love. Sometimes it is the enemy's plan to make us suffer more in sickness by robbing us of our faith. So whenever you are ill, whether it is something serious or just a cold or the flu, remember that Jesus is with you. Set your thoughts on Him, and ask Him to comfort you and bring you peace.

....

....

....

....

....

....

....

....

....

....

....

....

....

....

....

....

10

THE COMFORTS OF HOME

Dear Jesus,

As I sat rocking my little one, I began thinking of all the little comforts You bring to our home.

It's the little things here that comfort me, things like waking up to warm sunshine streaming through the bedroom window. The sound of birds singing and the aroma of fresh-brewed coffee, my spouse's gentle hug, my children's giggles, even the dog's sloppy kisses. All of them remind me: there's no place like home. When we sit down together to share a meal, and when we read bedtime stories, the comfort I feel is Your presence all around us.

Jesus, You are here with us all the time, providing for our needs. You have given us a strong shelter to live in, strong not only in its walls, but also in Your love. You provide food for our table and light in the darkness. And You even comfort us with Your grace and mercy on those days when we are grumpy with each other.

Thank You, Lord, for being here and bringing comfort into our home. I can't imagine living here without You!

In the multitude of my thoughts within me thy comforts delight my soul.—Psalm 94:19 KJV

Have you given thought to how Jesus makes your house a home? Look around for all the little things you might have missed, things you might have taken for granted. Some people refer to them as "creature comforts," but in truth they are Christ comforts! He is the one who makes your home the best place on earth.

....
....
....
....
....
....
....
....
....
....
....
....
....
....
....
....
....
....

REFLECTIONS ON COMFORT

REFLECTIONS ON COMFORT

JESUS,
I NEED
YOUR . . .

GRACE

1

THAT ONE DIFFICULT PERSON

Dear Jesus,

I need Your help. Someone is making my life very difficult. You know who it is. I don't need to tell You the name. I'm trying to understand why this person dislikes me. I have done my best to be kind and patient, but sometimes it's so hard. I've lost my temper, Lord, and I've said unkind things. We need healing. My relationship with this person is in need of much repair.

Jesus, show me what to do. I pray for You to intervene. Teach me Your way of dealing with this person. Help me shed my feelings of anger and hurt and replace them with love.

"Seventy times seven." That's what You said to Peter when he asked how many times he should forgive one who sins against him. Am I capable of forgiving that many times? I hope so. Help me stay strong, Lord. Help me forgive.

Bless this difficult person. Bless them day and night. Bless them with Your mercy and fill them with Your love. If anyone can warm their stone-cold heart, Jesus, You can.

Help us, please. We need You.

If it is possible, as far as it depends on you, live at peace with everyone.—Romans 12:18

At some point in your life, you will encounter a difficult person—someone who, no matter what you do, makes your life miserable. When you run into such a person, call on Jesus. He understands, and He knows just how to help. Go to Him in prayer and ask Him to intervene.

PATIENCE

Dear Jesus,

The world moves so fast that I find it hard to slow down and wait. I don't like it, Jesus, when something is out of my control and I'm forced to wait until whatever it is gets resolved. It's like being stuck in a traffic jam where I can't move. An obstacle gets in my way, and life stops.

Jesus, You are always so patient with me. You are patient when You teach me, and You are patient when it takes me awhile to learn. You are patient when my faith in You wanes, and You are even patient with my impatience! I want to be more like You. When things get in my way, I want to be able to say, and mean it, "Lord, I know that You've got this. You'll work it out. I'll just slow down, be calm, and wait on You."

I need You, Jesus. Please calm me down. Slow me down. Lead me to be more patient.

Wait for the Lord; be strong and take heart
and wait for the Lord. —Psalm 27:14

Waiting is hard work, often harder than work itself. When life throws a roadblock in your way, it's the perfect opportunity to practice patience. Seek God's will through prayer. Remember that His timing is always perfect. When you are forced to wait, think of it as a gift: God saying to you, "Not yet. I know what's up ahead."

....

....

....

....

....

....

....

....

....

....

....

....

....

....

....

....

....

3

THE POWER OF COMMUNITY

Dear Jesus,

Thank You for my church friends. I'm grateful that You've blessed me with a community of like-minded people who love You as I do.

Jesus, You have taught me that there is power in a community of believers. We pray and study the Bible together, and we enjoy finding ways to show others how much You love them. Together, we are stronger in our faith and more able to share You with the world. You watch over us and make us aware of needs that we otherwise might miss. Faithfully You lead us as Your disciples, giving us a heart for people near and far. When You show us a need, You help us fill it.

Jesus, You have shown me that I am just one piece of a big puzzle. When You put me together with my church friends, our ideas interlock to create a bigger picture of how we can serve You.

Thank You, Jesus! Please continue to bless us.

So in Christ we, though many, form
one body, and each member belongs
to all the others.—Romans 12:5

When Jesus lived on earth, He did not carry out His ministry alone. He enlisted disciples to help Him. Jesus' community of disciples continues to grow. Today, in churches throughout the world, groups of disciples come together to share God's Word, pray, and help fill the needs of others. Are you part of a Christian community?

4
LOVING THOSE WHO HATE

Dear Jesus,

Sometimes it's really hard to love people, particularly when You ask me to love those who hate You and do evil things. Please show me. How can I hate evil and still love the haters?

Isn't that what Paul did when he was in prison? In the worst of circumstances, he hated evil but continued to love. And You did the same, Jesus. When You were beaten, mocked, and crucified, You asked God to forgive Your enemies because they didn't know what they were doing. That is pure love.

Jesus, You are always in my heart, guiding me and leading me to be more like You. And for that reason, I have to pray for those who hate You and do evil things. I don't love what they do, Lord—but I want them to know You, so I pray for them. I love them enough to ask that You will save them. Please, Lord Jesus, come into their hearts. Open their eyes to see You. They need You so much.

"You have heard that it was said, 'Love your neighbor and hate your enemy.' But I tell you, love your enemies and pray for those who persecute you."—Matthew 5:43–44

When Jesus was on the cross, He prayed for His enemies and asked God to forgive them. Can you love someone who hates the Lord or who willingly inflicts suffering? Love doesn't mean that you accept acts of hatred and evil, but love requires that you pray for those most in need of salvation. Remember them when you pray.

....

....

....

....

....

....

....

....

....

....

....

....

....

....

....

....

....

5

JUST BECAUSE

Dear Jesus,

My children's comments and questions make me think. Sometimes when they ask me a question, I don't have a good answer. They ask things like, "Why do zebras have stripes?" and "How come dogs bark instead of meow?" I can only answer those questions, "Just because." My children accept that. For them "just because" is a good enough answer. That's the awesome thing about children—they can accept what's ambiguous and move on.

I wish that I had that kind of childlike faith. When You answer my why questions with "just because," I want a more concrete answer. Why didn't You heal that person's illness? Why did You allow that terrible thing to happen? It's difficult for me to accept by faith that some things just are.

Jesus, You have an answer to every question, but when You answer me with "just because," remind me to react like my children would. Some things are beyond my understanding.

"As the heavens are higher than the earth, so are my ways higher than your ways and my thoughts than your thoughts."—Isaiah 55:9

When you ask Jesus a question, He expects you to trust that His answer is perfectly right in every way. Sometimes He will speak an answer directly into your heart, and other times you will find it in God's Word, the Bible. There are some answers that He will not reveal. When He answers, "Just because," trust Him with a childlike faith. Some thoughts are His alone.

....

....

....

....

....

....

....

....

....

....

....

....

....

....

....

....

6

ANGELS IN DISGUISE

Dear Jesus,

In my times of greatest need, You sent people to help me. Some were family, friends, and neighbors, but many were strangers. I call Your human helpers "angels." They stop whatever they are doing to meet the needs of others, selflessly.

I see Your angels everywhere, Jesus. Some are doctors, nurses, and hospital chaplains. Others work in homeless shelters and serve meals to the poor. They help the elderly, sick, and lonely, and whenever there is an emergency these angels appear out of nowhere to help however they can.

Every day You send ordinary people to meet the needs of others. Sometimes they know that they are on a mission to help You, but most of the time You prefer to work quietly through them, leaving them unaware that they've made a difference in someone's life.

You know who they are, Jesus, these angel helpers of Yours. They shy away from recognition, so please bless them and show them how much they are loved.

Do not forget to show hospitality to strangers, for by so doing some people have shown hospitality to angels without knowing it. —Hebrews 13:2

Real angels do exist, but most of the time the Lord uses human helpers to meet specific needs. He works through missionaries, pastors, community leaders, neighbors, strangers—everyone! Be aware that whenever you act with kindness or offer encouragement, you are an angel-helper. Jesus is using you to fill someone's need.

7
REWARDS

Dear Jesus,

I believe that You exist and that You reward those who earnestly seek You. I seek You every day, Lord, and Your rewards are all around me. They fill me up with joy.

You reward me with peace in the middle of chaos, contentment when I need more, hope in brokenness, patience in adversity, and courage when I am afraid. You are loyal to me when others are not. Your love dries my tears, and Your strength lifts me up. I want for nothing because You give me what I need. When I ask, You hear me, and You bless me with Your best.

With mercy and grace, You reward me, although I am undeserving. And because I believe in You, death has no meaning. My life is eternal with Your promise of heaven. Knowing You as my Companion, Teacher, and Savior fills my heart with happiness.

Jesus, You are my all—my best reward.

And without faith it is impossible to please
God, because anyone who comes to him must
believe that he exists and that he rewards
those who earnestly seek him.—Hebrews 11:6

Knowing Jesus brings you joy. He is always faithful to those who believe in His existence and earnestly seek Him. It pleases Jesus when you invite Him into your heart. When you put your faith in Him He will reward you by giving you His best. What is your relationship with Jesus? Do you believe and trust in Him?

8

GUILT VS. GRACE

Dear Jesus,

Every day God showers His grace on me, providing me with things that I know I don't deserve. When He blesses me with something wonderful, I feel a pang of guilt. I look around at people suffering, and I ask myself, "Why does He bless me so much while other sinners suffer?" There is that part of me, still, that believes I have to earn God's grace.

Jesus, I know that the day I trusted in You, I received God's ultimate no-strings-attached love! Grace saved me from sin and gave me eternal life. Grace gives me strength and guides me. Grace blesses me with things that I know I don't deserve. Grace says, "God loves you!"

But how can I repay God for His immeasurable grace? I struggle with that.

As I pray this prayer, I hear You in my heart. You tell me, "Little one, you can never repay Me. All I ask is that you accept My grace without guilt. Love Me. Share My grace with others. Accept My gifts with joy!"

Jesus, I accept Your gifts without guilt. Lord, I love You! Thank You so much for grace.

But grow in the grace and knowledge of our Lord and Savior Jesus Christ. To him be glory both now and forever! Amen.—2 Peter 3:18

Grace is not earned. It is God's gift to you because He loves you. Paul says in Ephesians 2:8-9, "For it is by grace you have been saved, through faith—and this is not from yourselves, it is the gift of God—not by works, so that no one can boast." Guilt is appropriate only if you abuse God's grace by viewing it as a license to sin. Find joy in His grace, and use the ways He blesses you to bless others.

9

WHAT A MESS

Dear Jesus,

I have made a mess of things. I said and did things without thinking about what You would do and without seeking Your will. Now I've made things worse.

The situation was not mine. It belonged to her; it was hers to work through. My intentions were good, Jesus. I stepped in wanting to help, but I went about it the wrong way. I betrayed her confidence, shared her secret, and brought someone else into a private situation. I gave advice that was unsolicited and wrong. Now I am suffering from a very guilty conscience.

Jesus, I know that what I did was wrong, and I have been running from You since. I have asked her for forgiveness, and now I ask for Yours. Please forgive me for not turning to You for guidance. Forgive me for barging into a situation that was private, between You and her. Forgive me for thinking that I knew how to help better than You. Please, Jesus, take this guilty feeling away.

> "Come now, let us settle the matter," says the
> LORD. "Though your sins are like scarlet, they
> shall be as white as snow; though they are red
> as crimson, they shall be like wool."—Isaiah 1:18

Has the Lord used guilt to remind you that you are behaving outside of His will? It is always important to consult Him about solving a problem. Acting impulsively—even with good intentions—can sometimes create a mess. Forgiveness is a wonderful part of God's grace. When you have done something wrong, run to Him instead of away. If you come to Him with a sincere heart and confess your sins, He will forgive you.

10
FAITH AND GRACE

Dear Jesus,

You have taught me that faith and grace go hand in hand. Whenever I put my faith in You, I am rewarded with Your grace, and Your grace is always sufficient to meet my needs.

Often grace does not come in ways I expect. It comes quickly, a surprise ending to a test of faith. It may not exceed my needs, but it is always enough. Whether it is a basic need like food, clothing, and shelter, or a bigger need—mending a broken relationship, overcoming a financial burden, dealing with a health issue—You always hear my prayers. You see my faith unshaken as I rely on Your perfect will, and You reward me with Your abundant grace.

Your lessons on grace came to me hard. It took practice for me to trust You so fully and completely. But I have learned that when I put my trust in You, I am able to see Your grace more clearly, and Your grace never fails.

But he said to me, "My grace is sufficient for you, for my power is made perfect in weakness."—2 Corinthians 12:9

Having faith in the Lord's grace comes from recognizing and appreciating His gifts to you. Charles Spurgeon said, "Soar back through all your own experiences. Think of how the Lord has led you in the wilderness and has fed and clothed you every day. . . . Think of how the Lord's grace has been sufficient for you in all your troubles."[7] Do it today. Think of His gifts of grace, and then, with faith, put your trust in Him.

REFLECTIONS ON GRACE

REFLECTIONS ON GRACE

JESUS,
I NEED
YOU . . .

WHEN I FEEL DISAPPOINTMENT

1

THIS MIXED-UP WORLD

Dear Jesus,

I feel angry today. I'm disappointed with this scattered, mixed-up world. Everything seems turned upside down. What You've taught as wrong is often perceived as right. There are those who give new meaning to God's Word to fit what they want instead of what God wants from them. You are not welcome in many schools and public places anymore. If You knock, their doors are locked up tight. People hurt each other, Jesus. They hurt each other's bodies and they hurt each other's hearts. Everywhere I look there is fighting and discord, and bad news outweighs the good.

You mean so much to me. I want the whole world to know You and follow You. I do my best to tell others about Your goodness. I pray every day for all the world's nations and its leaders. But sometimes that just doesn't seem like enough. Please help me rise above my anger and find productive, peaceful ways to lead others to You.

"Therefore go and make disciples of all nations, baptizing them in the name of the Father and of the Son and of the Holy Spirit, and teaching them to obey everything I have commanded you. And surely I am with you always, to the very end of the age."—Matthew 28:19–20

The world can be a difficult place for Christians. This is nothing new. The Bible holds many stories of wars, persecution, and fighting. But in every situation God wins! He is always triumphant. When the world appears mixed up and scattered, remember that you are Jesus' disciple. Give the anger and disappointment to Him, and allow Him to work His goodness through you.

2

BACK TO YOU

Dear Jesus,

There was a time when my partner and I both loved You, but now my partner has fallen away from his faith. You know the circumstances, Lord. You know what happened that made him lose trust in You. It disappoints me to be married to someone who can't see that You are with us even when bad things happen.

While my partner drifts away from You, I feel closer to You than ever. I rely on You every day to get us over this rough spot. But, Jesus, I need You to help me stay encouraged and strong. I know that You are still in my partner's heart. I believe that he will come back to You someday. I just wish that it would happen sooner rather than later. I want us both to walk hand in hand with You, to pray and read the Bible together as we did so often.

Come, Lord Jesus. Heal the heart of the one I love. Bring him back to You and to me.

"*I will search for the lost and bring back the strays. I will bind up the injured and strengthen the weak.*"—*Ezekiel 34:16*

When your partner is searching and questioning his faith, try to focus on your own relationship with Jesus. Trust that He knows every little detail of why your spouse has fallen away. Jesus hears your partner's unspoken questions, and He sees when your partner wrestles with God. Trust Jesus today, one day at a time. Pray for Him to lead your spouse home.

3

JESUS, I TRIED SO HARD!

Dear Jesus,

I tried so hard to make it work, but I failed. This situation didn't end the way that I had hoped and expected it would, and I am so disappointed.

I sought Your will, and I thought I knew what to do. I used great care moving forward toward the goal, and I stopped often to pray. When obstacles got in my way, I asked for Your guidance, and I waited patiently for You to answer me. I was diligent in my work, never giving up. And then, with the finish line in sight, everything came crashing down. All of my work was for nothing! I am like the runner who has trained for a marathon. I ran fast and hard and then, just a few yards from the finish line, I fell.

Why, Jesus? Why did You allow me to work so hard and get so close just so I would fail?

> *I have fought the good fight, I have finished the race, I have kept the faith.* —2 Timothy 4:7

Disappointment makes us ask, "Why didn't I? Why didn't God?" Sometimes the Lord allows disappointment in order to build our faith. The apostle Paul is an example. Few worked harder than he, but all his hard work landed him in prison. Paul's disappointment strengthened his faith and drew him nearer to the Lord. When disappointment strikes, keep the faith. Remember—Jesus loves you!

4

TRYING TO BE PERFECT

Dear Jesus,

I am so frustrated and disappointed in myself. I want to be better than I am, and I want to do bigger and greater things. I know that I am not all that I can be. When I was in school, I wanted to be at the top of my class, but I wasn't. Someone was smarter than I was. At work, I am passed over for promotions although I want to move up and am the hardest worker in my department. And at home, I can't keep up with my household chores and the demands put on me by my family. It causes me such stress!

Jesus, You never made mistakes. Everything You did was perfect and good. I want to be just like You. That is what I pray for daily—to be like You and to be the very best at everything I set out to do.

Jesus, I need You. Will You help me?

Let us keep looking to Jesus. He is
the author of faith. He also makes
it perfect.—Hebrews 12:2 NIRV

It is good to want to be "just like Jesus," but remember, He is God and the only One who is absolutely perfect. If you feel disappointed in yourself because you expect perfection, re-visit your goals. To be perfect isn't what the Lord wants from you. You don't have to be the best at everything. What's more important is having faith in Jesus to lead you where He needs you most. Make that your daily prayer.

....

....

....

....

....

....

....

....

....

....

....

....

....

....

....

....

5

JESUS, DO I DISAPPOINT YOU?

Dear Jesus,

My youngest child has been misbehaving all week, and my patience with her has worn thin. Today she played quietly, and after a while she said, "Mommy, I'm trying to be better. So are you still disappointed in me?" I took her in my arms and reassured her that no matter how much she misbehaved, I will always love her. When I did that, Jesus, You spoke to my heart.

Like my little girl, I sometimes misbehave. Just like everyone else, I am a sinner. I've wondered: Are You disappointed in me? At times I've avoided coming to You in prayer because I've felt guilty about something that I've done. I didn't want to face You. Instead, I acted like my daughter, quiet and good, trying to work up the courage to come to You and be reassured of Your love.

Today you reminded me that You are my loving Father. I don't know why I worry, because I know that You love me! Nothing I could ever do will change that. So forgive me, Lord, for avoiding You, and thank You for loving me even when I disappoint You.

Neither death nor life, neither angels nor demons, neither the present nor the future, nor any powers, neither height nor depth, nor anything else in all creation, will be able to separate us from the love of God that is in Christ Jesus our Lord.—Romans 8:38–39

You never have to run from Jesus when you've done something wrong. First John 1:9 says, "If we confess our sins, he is faithful and just and will forgive us our sins and purify us from all unrighteousness." Jesus loves you all the time—forever—and nothing can change that.

....

....

....

....

....

....

....

....

....

....

....

....

....

....

....

....

....

6

UNDERAPPRECIATED

Dear Jesus,

Is it wrong for me to feel underappreciated? Every time I find wayward socks strewn in the hallway or pick up a toy that I've tripped over, I wonder if my family appreciates me.

When I'm just finishing making a nice dinner, and my husband calls to say that he's going to be at least an hour late, and my kids look at the meal I've prepared and say, "What's that?" am I wrong to feel like they don't care?

In the first years of our marriage, my husband loved everything that I did. He'd compliment me on my cooking and even thank me for preparing his favorite meals. It's been quite awhile since I've heard him say, "Thank you." And when the kids were little, they'd say, "You're the best mommy ever!" They'd shower me with hugs and kisses. Now my oldest barely grunts, "Hello."

Jesus, I'm disappointed. I know that married couples settle into their routines and kids begin to pull away when they get older, but I miss those days when Mommy felt loved.

> *"So . . . do not be dismayed, for I am your God. I will strengthen you and help you; I will uphold you with my righteous right hand."*—Isaiah 41:10

Working, maintaining a household, and meeting the needs of a spouse and children take all of the energy, strength, and courage that a woman can muster. No wonder wives and mothers sometimes feel less than appreciated. If you feel that way, draw your strength from the Lord and remember that He values and loves you. Then gently remind your family that Mommy needs a little tender loving care.

7

DISAPPOINTED CHILDREN

Dear Jesus,

It hurts me to see my children disappointed, but there are times when I must say no to what they want—and most often it is for their own good.

If I gave in every time my kids wanted to eat sweets, I might have sick children. And if I bought them everything they wanted, they might be spoiled. When I won't allow them to play at a new friend's house before I've met the parents, I do it because I want them always to be safe. Lord, they are too young to understand any of this. All they know is that Mommy said no, and that makes them disappointed and sad.

I empathize with how they feel, because I am sometimes disappointed when You say no to me. Yet I understand that when You turn me down, it is for my good, either to keep me safe and sound, or else because You have something better planned for me.

Dear Jesus, help me always do what's best for my kids, even if it disappoints them and makes me sad.

My son, listen to your father's advice. Don't turn away from your mother's teaching. What they teach you will be like a beautiful crown on your head. It will be like a chain to decorate your neck.—Proverbs 1:8–9 NIRV

Do you find it hard to say no to your children? Imagine what chaos there would be if you said yes to your children all the time in every circumstance! Children need guidance and protection. Jesus knows that. And He knows, too, that parents also need to be told no. Like every good parent, God says no for our own good. He does not always give us what we want, but He always gives us what we need.

....
....
....
....
....
....
....
....
....
....
....
....
....
....
....
....
....

8

REJOICE IN DISAPPOINTMENT?

Dear Jesus,

The apostle Paul said to rejoice in suffering because it gives us strength and builds our character, but that is much easier said than done. How can I be happy when disappointment stings me so hard? I have nothing to rejoice about. I did my best, and I expected to win. I might be able to muster just a tiny smidge of rejoicing and give myself some credit, but only because in the midst of the shock and disappointment of losing I managed to act like a good loser. I congratulated my opponent with a smile and a hug. Rejoice!

Jesus, I have a bad attitude right now. My displeasure is waging war inside me with what I know to be right—to gracefully accept what happened and move on.

Why is that so hard, Lord? Why can't I just say, "Oh well," and hope that next time I will do better?

Be of good courage, and he shall strengthen your heart, all ye that hope in the LORD.—Psalm 31:24 KJV

Disappointment can be a tough thing to swallow. Sometimes all you can do with disappointment is to endure it and have hope. Hope for what? Hope for better things to come, for motivation to try again, and to eventually let go of your disappointment. But most of all, hope in Jesus! He will get you through the hard times and help you move on.

....

....

....

....

....

....

....

....

....

....

....

....

....

....

....

....

....

9

COURAGE TO TRY AGAIN

Dear Jesus,

I've failed again. I thought that after so many tries I had finally found the missing piece. I believed that this time I knew how to succeed. But I was wrong.

I feel like giving up. The road to success is long, hard, and filled with mountains to climb and valleys to rise up from. I'm tired. Disappointment says stop trying. Jesus, I doubt that I have the strength or the courage to try one more time. Yet there is a place deep within me saying, "Continue on. Keep going." Is that Your voice, Lord? Is that what You want me to do?

I have never been a quitter. I have always managed to pull myself up from defeat and try again. A small part of me is still willing, but I need You to help me. Will You please give me strength? Jesus, will You give me courage to look beyond this disappointment and try again?

There is surely a future hope for you, and your hope will not be cut off.—Proverbs 23:18

The great Martin Luther King Jr. said, "We must accept finite disappointment, but we must never lose infinite hope."[8] And where does one find "infinite hope"? In Jesus! If you find yourself disappointed again and again and losing hope, then call on Jesus for help. He will give you the courage and strength to let go of your disappointment and try again.

10

YOU NEVER DISAPPOINT ME

Dear Jesus,

Whatever would I do without You? You never disappoint me or let me down. Day and night, every day and forever, You are the one who watches over me, protects me, leads me, and loves me. Oh, Jesus, You are so wonderful!

When I am weak, You make me strong. When I am knocked down, You pick me up. Your words soothe and comfort me, and Your example sets me on the right path. When I need to decide, You are the one who makes me wise. You are always with me. You speak to my heart. You wake me in the morning and tuck me in at night.

Jesus, when the world disappoints me, when life throws obstacles in my way, it doesn't matter because You are my God. Nothing can ever come between us. I know that always You are there working on my behalf, doing for me, with Your perfect knowledge, what is right and good and best.

Dear Jesus, I love You!

"I am the Lord; those who hope in me will not be disappointed."—Isaiah 49:23

Because there is sin in the world, there is disappointment. You can't escape being disappointed sometimes, but when that happens you can rely on this: Jesus will never disappoint you or let you down. His love for you is unconditional, and when you put your faith in Him, you can be sure that He will work out every setback and problem for your good.

....
....
....
....
....
....
....
....
....
....
....
....
....
....
....
....
....

REFLECTIONS ON DISAPPOINTMENT

....

....

....

....

....

....

....

....

....

....

....

....

....

....

....

....

....

....

....

....

....

....

REFLECTIONS ON DISAPPOINTMENT

....

....

....

....

....

....

....

....

....

....

....

....

....

....

....

....

....

....

....

....

....

JESUS,
I NEED
YOUR . . .

FAITH
AND HOPE

1

THE LIGHT OF MY LIFE

Dear Jesus,

Thank You for the gift of light and the joy it brings me.

Sometimes I get up early to watch the sun rise. Patiently I wait while the velvet night yields to smoky gray and the eastern sky turns gold. Through God's faithfulness, the sun appears each morning, bringing warmth and light to my brand-new day.

Jesus, You light up my life all day. You said, "I am the light of the world. Whoever follows me will never walk in darkness, but will have the light of life" (John 8:12). All day long, Your light is with me. Your love brightens even the darkest days. All around me, I see bright little miracles—You turning darkness to light.

When evening comes, I watch the sun set. The western sky is ablaze with fiery colors, a brilliant show before You dim the lights and turn on the moon and stars. In the glow of the moonlight, You watch over me while I sleep.

Oh, Jesus—all day, all night, You are the light of my life.

"I have come into the world as a light, so that no one who believes in me should stay in darkness."—John 12:46

Hippolytus, a third-century theologian, said, "A heavenly light more brilliant than all others sheds its radiance everywhere, and he who was begotten before the morning star and all the stars of heaven, Christ . . . shines upon all creatures more brightly than the sun."[9] Jesus is the light of the world. Notice how brightly He shines in your life today.

....

....

....

....

....

....

....

....

....

....

....

....

....

....

....

....

....

WHEN I ASK

Dear Jesus,

You are amazing. Not only do You give me what I need, but You provide substantially more than I ask for.

In Matthew 7:9–11, You say, "Which of you, if your son asks for bread, will give him a stone? Or if he asks for a fish, will give him a snake? If you, then, though you are evil, know how to give good gifts to your children, how much more will your Father in heaven give good gifts to those who ask him!" That means when I ask You for something, You already know if it's good for me. If I ask amiss, You have something better planned, and what I receive from You will be even greater than what I've asked for.

Jesus, remind me not to limit You by requesting what I need, but by asking for Your will to be done. If I ask in faith and I believe in Your goodness, I know that I will receive exactly what I need and something better than I can imagine.

Now to him who is able to do immeasurably more than all we ask or imagine, according to his power that is at work within us.—Ephesians 3:20

Could it be that you expect too little from God? Think carefully about what you want, and don't be afraid to pray for something big. Ask God to take your request and refine it according to what He knows is good for you. Then expect Him to answer, exceeding your expectations. God is your perfect, loving Father, and He will give you His best.

....

....

....

....

....

....

....

....

....

....

....

....

....

....

....

....

3
COURAGE

Dear Jesus,

I want to be more courageous. I need to be unafraid to step out in faith and follow You. I feel You tugging at my heart, telling me that You want me to do more with the gifts You have given me. I confess, Jesus: that makes me afraid.

I'm comfortable just the way that I am. You know that I don't like change. Change is scary. It's facing my fear of the unknown. I want to know absolutely and certainly what I am walking into.

But You don't work that way.

You want me to step forward in faith and trust that Your plans for me are good. "Come," You say, "Walk with Me." But I am like a child afraid to take her father's hand and go with him into the darkness.

Jesus, give me the courage to trust You more and to grab tightly to Your hand. Guide me gently. Strengthen me so I can be all that You want me to be.

"For I am the LORD your God who takes hold of your right hand and says to you, Do not fear; I will help you."—Isaiah 41:13

The uncertainty that comes with change can produce anxiety and resistance. It takes courage to move forward with faith into the unknown. Jesus is the one who can provide that courage. If you hear Him calling you to do something new, listen. Trust Him and take His hand. His plan for you is good. He will help you.

4

YOU ARE MY HOPE

Dear Jesus,

You are the source of my hope. You give me hope when I rise in the morning, hope of a brand-new day, a clean slate ready to be filled with the best of me. Your hope motivates me to work hard and have confidence that I will meet the day's goals and challenges.

You give me hope at midday when I feel stressed as life presses down on me hard. When I ask You to renew my strength and calm my racing mind, I know that You will. You are always present with me, helping me throughout my day, renewing me so that I might strive to accomplish good things.

In the evening, You give me hope of an even better tomorrow. You forgive me for the mistakes that I have made today and wipe my slate clean.

Jesus, all the days of my life, my hope lies in You. And when my days here are done, I have one more hope—the hope of life with You forever.

Now faith is confidence in what we hope for and assurance about what we do not see.—Hebrews 11:1

Hope is the reason for believing that something you desire will be fulfilled. Jesus is Hope. He hears your prayers and is ready to answer. By making Him the source of your hope, you can be confident of receiving His best for you. Pray and make your hopes known to Him, then believe by faith that He will bless you with exactly what you need.

....

....

....

....

....

....

....

....

....

....

....

....

....

....

....

....

....

....

5

HOPE IS A GIFT

Dear Jesus,

Some days I have to remind myself that hope is a gift. It comes from You, and all You ask for in return is faith.

I remember a time in my life before I knew You when I felt hopeless. It was the worst feeling, lonely and vulnerable. My future looked bleak because I had no hope. But, Jesus, when I found You, all of that changed. As I learned to trust You, hope grew inside me and, finally, the future looked bright.

There are still times when I doubt that I will receive what I ask for in prayer—I'm only human, after all—but then I read my Bible, and You renew my hope. I have faith and trust in You! I will be strong and wait for You to answer me.

Jesus, my hope is in You. What a gift it is believing that You are real and that You love me. You hear my prayers, and You will answer. You know what I've asked for, and You will give me what's best.

Why, my soul, are you downcast? Why so disturbed within me? Put your hope in God, for I will yet praise him, my Savior and my God.—Psalm 42:11

Hopelessness is a hollow feeling that can only be cured by a healthy dose of faith. When you put all your faith in Jesus, He gives you the gift of hope. Reread the gospels and study Christ's character. Everything He did was good. He never lied. Jesus is perfect in every way, and He will answer all of your prayers perfectly, with your best interests in mind. Have faith in Him, trust Him, and never lose hope.

....

....

....

....

....

....

....

....

....

....

....

....

....

....

....

....

6

TRY, TRY AGAIN

Dear Jesus,

I am like a baby learning to walk. I fall down often, but I always get up and try again. But unlike a child, I know that I can do almost anything because my hope is in You.

Jesus, when the enemy shouts, "Give it up," You whisper to me, "Try it one more time."

Your soft, sweet voice lifts me high above discouragement. It keeps despair from creeping in. You motivate me to try new things that some people might think are beyond what I'm able to do. My expectation soars because You and I both know that I can accomplish great things as long as I stay firm in my hope.

Jesus, some people call me stubborn. Others say that I am determined. But I tell them that I am just hopeful. And if they ask why, I quote the apostle Paul: "I can do all this through him who gives me strength" (Philippians 4:13).

Jesus, You make everything possible. Thank You for giving me hope!

"Nothing is impossible with God."—Luke 1:37 NIRV

The poet Emily Dickinson wrote this description of hope: "'Hope' is the thing with feathers / That perches in the soul / And sings the tune without the words / And never stops at all."[10] What a lovely way to describe hope in Jesus! His hope is uplifting yet always settled in your soul, singing to you softly: "Run the good race. Don't give up. Something wonderful awaits you at the finish line."

....

....

....

....

....

....

....

....

....

....

....

....

....

....

....

....

7
THINGS UNSEEN

Dear Jesus,

I have a hard time hoping in things I cannot see. For me, hope comes easy when life goes my way. But as soon as obstacles block my path, hope turns murky, and my future is opaque. Jesus, I need You. Please increase my hope.

How can I believe in You and then not hope in things unseen? I have never seen You, yet I believe in You because of what I read in the Bible. I believe because I feel You in my heart. I know that You are there. In the past when I've had no hope, You still brought me through valleys and lifted me up onto mountaintops. Why isn't that enough to make me stand firm in hope, believing that I will receive Your best for me?

Jesus, a piece is missing. I need to complete the connection between You and this elusive thing called hope. *Will You help me?*

But hope that is seen is no hope at all. Who
hopes for what they already have? But if
we hope for what we do not yet have, we
wait for it patiently.—Romans 8:24–25

That missing piece is *faith*. If you haven't read Hebrews 11 lately, then visit that chapter today. It begins, "Now faith is confidence in what we hope for and assurance about what we do not see." The examples in this chapter show hopeful people putting faith into action. Did they always receive what they hoped for? No. Often they received something better. Remember—faith is the thing that builds up hope.

....

....

....

....

....

....

....

....

....

....

....

....

....

....

....

....

8

FAITHFUL RELATIONSHIPS

Dear Jesus,

I want to be more trusting, and that means making better choices. In the past, I have chosen poorly and been with people who hurt me and let me down. That not only destroyed my faith in people in general, but it also made me lose faith in myself. Honestly? The only one I trust now is You.

My hope is that You will show me how to choose the best people for me—people who truly love and care for not only me but also You! That is my prayer, Jesus. That You will help me choose wisely and build my trust in people again.

I know that You are the only one whom I can trust fully and completely (none of us humans are perfect, after all), but surely, Lord, there have to be some new friends out there for me who love You and are worthy of my trust.

Jesus, You are my hope. I need You. Please help me trust again.

Do not be joined to unbelievers. What do right and wrong have in common? Can light and darkness be friends?—2 Corinthians 6:14 NIRV

Has your faith in people been shaken? Then maybe you aren't making wise choices. The Bible says that we should not team up with unbelievers. Does that mean there isn't a place for them in your life? No. But it does mean that you should choose your close friends wisely. Ask Jesus to be your matchmaker. When you follow His lead, you will be assured of a match made in heaven!

....

....

....

....

....

....

....

....

....

....

....

....

....

....

....

....

9

HOPE FOR MY CHILDREN

Dear Jesus,

I give my children to You. I give them to You fully with the strong hope that You will grow them into adults who love You and also trust in Your love for them.

There will be bumps and bruises along the way and, I expect, some deep valleys. Those are all inescapable parts of childhood, growing up, and learning. But, Jesus, please keep my children from giving in to the really bad stuff: gangs, drugs, alcohol, crime, sex. Be in their hearts always and speak to them in a loud, firm voice. Protect them from evil and guide the choices they make.

I suppose that there will be times when they wholly disagree with me and times when I think that they don't love me. When that happens, Jesus, strengthen my faith and hope in You. This parenting job is not an easy one, and I need You to help me. I believe that You will.

> People were bringing little children to Jesus
> for him to place his hands on them, but the
> disciples rebuked them. When Jesus saw
> this, he was indignant. He said to them,
> "Let the little children come to me, and do
> not hinder them, for the kingdom of God
> belongs to such as these."—Mark 10:13–14

One of the best gifts that you can give to Jesus, and to your-self, is entrusting your children to Him. It's not an easy gift to give. It means that although you will do your very best raising your children, you have put Jesus in complete control of their futures. Doing that takes faith. It requires that you trust Jesus with the most precious things in your life. Can you do it? Pray and ask Him to help you.

....

....

....

....

....

....

....

....

....

....

....

....

....

....

....

....

....

10

HOPE IS ETERNAL

Dear Jesus,

I read a book recently about the king of Prussia in the 1700s, Frederick the Great. He said, "The time I live in is a time of turmoil. My hope is in God."[11] His quotation, Lord, reminded me that hope in You is eternal. Life goes on and changes, but hope in You doesn't change—ever.

From long before King Frederick's time until right now, the world's people have suffered from misplaced hope. In times of turmoil, they've centered their hope on leaders, on armies with powerful weapons, and on political parties and organizations. Sometimes their hopes were realized, and sometimes they failed. But always, the people and things where hope once was have passed into history. The only true and sustained hope, Jesus, is You.

Lord, we need Your help. Please open the eyes and hearts of our world's leaders; teach them the powerful lesson in Frederick the Great's quotation. In this time of turmoil, the world's hope must be in You.

> *Do any of the worthless idols of the nations bring rain? Do the skies themselves send down showers? No, it is you, LORD our God. Therefore our hope is in you, for you are the one who does all this.—Jeremiah 14:22*

History holds valuable lessons. The Bible is, in one sense, a history book. It tells the history of man: what happens when man puts faith and hope in God, and what happens when he doesn't. The history of our world teaches us lessons too. One of them is that God's will always prevails, and for those who stand firm in their faith, hope is eternal. Where is your hope centered today? In turmoil, is Jesus your hope?

....

....

....

....

....

....

....

....

....

....

....

....

....

....

....

....

REFLECTIONS ON FAITH & HOPE

REFLECTIONS ON FAITH & HOPE

JESUS,
I NEED
YOUR . . .

WISDOM

1

TIME-OUT

Dear Jesus,

Several times I asked my child to do something, and he kept saying no. So I gave him a time-out. Time-outs work. I've discovered that if I give my child enough of them, he eventually learns to do what I say. When I tell my son to do something, it's always for his own good, because I want him to grow into an adult who knows the difference between right and wrong. I want him to love and to follow You.

Jesus, when I gave my son his time-out, You reminded me of something. I am a child of God, and sometimes He gives me time-outs too. Like my little boy, I don't always listen. God gives me plenty of chances to hear and obey, but there are times when I go my own way. When I don't listen, God eventually does something to set my mind on what He wants me to do. He gives me a heavenly time-out!

I'm grateful, Jesus, that You reminded me of that. We grown-ups need time-outs too.

"Do not make light of the Lord's discipline,
and do not lose heart when he rebukes
you, because the Lord disciplines the
one he loves." —Hebrews 12:5–6

Isn't it wonderful that God sees us as His children? He wants us to grow strong in Him, and sometimes He nudges us with gentle discipline. When God gives you a time-out, it helps to pray, read your Bible, and listen to your heart. He is eager to teach you and eager for you to learn.

DEAD-END

Dear Jesus,

I was so sure. I thought I was following Your will and taking the path You chose for me. But then I came to a dead end. All of that time spent, the determination and hard work, has led to nothing. Jesus, how could I be so wrong? I prayed and asked You to lead me. I meditated on Scripture. In my heart, I thought I knew exactly which way You wanted me to go. But I was wrong.

What now?

I trust You, Jesus, but I'm standing still. I'm afraid to take another step forward. What if I choose the wrong path again? I don't want to waste more time, and I don't want to disappoint You. I wish that I had a map that showed exactly where You want me to go and how to get there. Jesus, I need You. Please show me the way.

Trust in the LORD with all your heart and lean not on your own understanding; in all your ways submit to him, and he will make your paths straight.—Proverbs 3:5–6

Jesus understands. He knows where you are going and how to get there, even when you don't. It is important to remember that a dead end may be a part of the plan the Lord has for you. Rather than view it as failure, concentrate on what you gained from following the path. Keep trusting Jesus. He loves you, and He will show you the way.

....

....

....

....

....

....

....

....

....

....

....

....

....

....

....

....

3

JESUS UNDERSTANDS

Dear Jesus,

Sometimes I behave badly. I don't mean to; it just happens. When I feel stressed out and overwhelmed, then I say and do things that I am ashamed of. I don't like this part of me. I've been trying to improve it.

Jesus, You know me so well. You understand my imperfections. You understand when I lose my temper and say things that I shouldn't or when I act out because I am afraid. When I behave badly, even when I don't understand it myself, You understand me.

Imperfection is part of being human, and I'm grateful, Jesus, that You forgive me and allow me opportunities to try again. I don't like the ways I behave sometimes, and I know that my bad behavior disappoints You.

Will You help me, please? When anger or fear tempt me to behave in ways that are not pleasing to You, help me stop and think before I speak or act.

For we do not have a high priest who is unable to empathize with our weaknesses, but we have one who has been tempted in every way, just as we are—yet he did not sin.—Hebrews 4:15

When feeling stressed out causes you to react in ways that leave you feeling guilty or ashamed, Jesus understands. Bad behavior is part of being human; still, being human is not an excuse for continuing to behave badly. Ask Jesus to help with your behavior. When you feel tempted to react in a negative way, keep your eyes on Him. Let Jesus be your example.

4

THE SECRET OF CONTENTMENT

Dear Jesus,

Please help me find contentment. As hard as I try, I struggle to find satisfaction in who I am and the things I try to accomplish.

In Philippians 4:12–13, the apostle Paul says, "I know what it is to be in need, and I know what it is to have plenty. I have learned the secret of being content in any and every situation, whether well fed or hungry, whether living in plenty or in want. I can do all this through him who gives me strength." Jesus, I want to learn Paul's secret too. Will You teach me?

I know that the secret lies in trust. I need to trust You more and trust myself less. Trust doesn't come easy for me, Lord, so be patient with me. Help me gain strength by trusting in You. Even in the worst of circumstances, Paul was content. I want that kind of contentment too. Please show me the way.

I have learned to be content whatever the circumstances.—Philippians 4:11

Paul said that he *learned* the secret of being content. Contentment doesn't just happen; it comes with nurturing your relationship with Jesus and allowing it to flourish. The secret to contentment is complete trust in the Lord. Pray and ask Jesus to help you find contentment through trusting in Him.

....

....

....

....

....

....

....

....

....

....

....

....

....

....

....

....

....

....

....

5

TRUE WISDOM

Dear Jesus,

Thanks to You, I have learned the true meaning of wisdom. Wisdom comes from studying the Bible, knowing You, and putting Your teachings into practice. People gain different degrees of wisdom based on how willing they are to dig in to Your teaching and apply it to their lives. The more that they read Your Word and understand it, the greater their wisdom becomes. And it is this wisdom learned from You that sets them free.

Jesus, You are helping me become wise. By studying the Bible and knowing Your views on what is right and wrong, I don't have to muddle through worldly decisions rife with Satan's tricks. Instead, I am able to make a decision quickly based on the wisdom that comes from You.

When I am not sure about something, the Bible is my textbook. I review Your promises and seek Your will, and I know that where my wisdom is lacking, You will provide me with Yours.

Thank You, Lord, for being so willing to teach me. Thank You for making me wise.

If any of you lacks wisdom, you should ask God, who gives generously to all without finding fault, and it will be given to you.—James 1:5

True wisdom cannot be found in textbooks. It comes with learning the right way to live in the world—and that knowledge comes from the Lord. Wisdom lives in the heart. It knows what is good and right and acts in that way. When put into action, it sets an example for others to follow. You are wise only if you are not just head smart, but also heart smart.

6

OPEN THEIR HEARTS

Dear Jesus,

This prayer is for my children. Please give me what I ask for. I want You to open my children's hearts to receive Your wisdom. I can't always be with them to make sure that they are behaving in a godly way and making decisions that are good, safe, and right. But You are with them always, Lord. So open up their hearts and pour Your wisdom in.

Jesus, I want them to recognize Your voice in their hearts, and not only recognize it but also pay attention to it. When You tell them no, I want them to stop whatever they are doing and follow You instead. When their peers try to get them to do something against what they know is right, I want them to be brave enough and wise enough to walk away.

We are doing our best as parents to raise children who love and live for You, but we need You to help us, especially during those times when they are beyond our sight.

Thank You, dear Jesus. I love You.

The LORD will watch over your coming and going both now and forevermore.—Psalm 121:8

What parent doesn't worry about their children when they are out of their sight? Even the best-taught children sometimes lack wisdom to make the best choices. That is why it is so important to ask Jesus to help with your parenting. Ask Him to teach your children to be wise in all that they do. Then trust Him to answer your prayer.

....

....

....

....

....

....

....

....

....

....

....

....

....

....

....

....

....

....

7

WISDOM IN THE STORM

Dear Jesus,

The sky has turned dark, and I am wrapped up in gray clouds swirling around me, a dense foggy mist. I cannot find my way. I call out to You, listen for Your voice, but I do not hear it. A cold rain pours down on me, and I have nowhere to go. Dear Jesus, tell me what to do. Give me wisdom to endure this storm.

I want to hide from my circumstances, but there is no place to run to. I want You to lead me, but where are You? Why is heaven so far away? Jesus, come to me. I need You.

There are only questions, no answers. I am consumed with worry and overwhelmed by fear. Each step I take is tentative. I am unsure of where I am, and I am afraid that I might fall.

Dear Jesus, You know exactly what I need, and You have the power to bring me in from the rain. Please come, Lord Jesus, I beg You.

> *Then they cried out to the LORD in their trouble,*
> *and he brought them out of their distress. He*
> *stilled the storm to a whisper.—Psalm 107:28–29*

Have you ever felt so desperate that you begged Jesus for help? Some situations require begging. They are harsh storms that come fast, hard, and unexpected. In that sort of intense storm, only the Lord can rescue you. He, in His wisdom, knows exactly where you are, and He knows the way to safety. If you find yourself in a storm, be strong in faith and trust Him. He will show you the way.

8

TO KNOW YOU

Dear Jesus,

As always, You have enlightened me through Your Word. I was reading Paul's letter to the Ephesians, and I was struck by this verse: "I keep asking that the God of our Lord Jesus Christ, the glorious Father, may give you the Spirit of wisdom and revelation, so that you may know him better" (Ephesians 1:17). Jesus, I understand now that when I've asked for wisdom in the past, I was not asking with the right purpose in mind.

Whenever I asked for wisdom, I was often looking for a solution to a problem. Sometimes You didn't give a clear answer and left the solution up to me. I never understood why. Now I realize that the real reason for asking for wisdom is to know You better. Through every answered request and every one that is met with silence, I learn more about You.

So, Lord, here is my request: in the future, whenever I ask for wisdom, please answer me in a way that will help me know You better.

Let the one who is wise heed these things and ponder the loving deeds of the Lord. —Psalm 107:43

There is wisdom in Paul's words. When you read through his books in the Bible, you will gain wisdom and insight into the character of God. In Ephesians, Paul shows us what kind of wisdom to ask for. When God answers a request for wisdom in an unexpected way or when He remains silent, ask Him, "Lord, what can I learn about You from this?" He will surely give you the wisdom needed to know Him better.

....

....

....

....

....

....

....

....

....

....

....

....

....

....

....

....

9
WISDOM TO HELP

Dear Jesus,

I need Your wisdom about how to get over a significant loss. I've experienced loss myself, Lord, many times—death of a loved one, losing a best friend, a job loss. And all the time You've brought me through it. But now, Jesus, I need to provide help to someone else, and just telling her, "Trust in the Lord," doesn't seem to be enough.

Jesus, what can I say and do to help my loved one through this very difficult time? I need You to provide me with just the right words at the right times. I need You to tell me when to step in and when to stay away. Will You please give me a glimpse into her heart, so I will know what she needs? And then, Lord, put in my heart the best way to help her.

You and I both know that You are enough, but my friend needs me too. Give me the wisdom to help her.

Carry each other's burdens, and in this way you will fulfill the law of Christ.—Galatians 6:2

When our loved ones hurt, we hurt too. Of course, Jesus is enough to overcome hurt all by Himself. But imagine if we all decided that because He is enough we should just sit back and do nothing. That's not what the Bible says! It holds countless examples of people helping each other and loving one another. When your loved one hurts, ask Jesus to show you what you can do to help ease their pain.

10

HIS MYSTERIOUS WAYS

Dear Jesus,

So much of what You do is a mystery. I ask myself, "Why is He sometimes silent? Why does He heal some people and not others? How can He be everywhere at the same time and love everyone despite their sins?" The only answer I have is because You, Jesus, are God's Son, God made flesh, the one whose ways are too wonderful for me to understand.

Your mystery intrigues me. Your timing is always perfect. Your answers to prayer are often confusing, an intricate weaving of fibers from heaven. Lord, You make things whole when shattered pieces are missing. You surprise me. Sometimes You frighten me because You are so unpredictable and uncontrollable. Your strength and power overwhelm me, and I am in awe of how mighty You are.

Even when Your divine mysteries are beyond my understanding, I put my faith and trust in You. My understanding is limited, but Your love for me is not. You are good and trustworthy, always!

Surely I spoke of things I did not understand, things too wonderful for me to know. —Job 42:3

Do you try to understand why God allows certain things? Do you ask Him why when He does something beyond your understanding? God sometimes answers our why questions with silence. Some things about Him are too wonderful or too complicated for a human mind to comprehend. Loving God means accepting His mysterious ways and knowing that He will meet your needs, now and forever.

....

....

....

....

....

....

....

....

....

....

....

....

....

....

....

....

....

REFLECTIONS ON WISDOM

REFLECTIONS ON WISDOM

NOTES

1. Corrie ten Boom, *Tramp for the Lord* (New York: Jove, 1978), 140.
2. "Judson W. Van DeVenter," *Hymnary.org*, accessed August 16, 2014, http://www.hymnary.org/person/VanDeVenter_JW.
3. Rev. Richard Briscoe Cook DD, *The Wit and Wisdom of Rev. Charles H. Spurgeon* (Baltimore: R. H. Woodward and Company, 1891), 330.
5. Anne Frank, *Anne Frank: The Diary of a Young Girl* (New York: Bantam, 1993), 171.
6. Martin Luther, quoted in *The Westminster Collection of Christian Quotations*, compiled by Martin H. Manser (Louisville, KY: Westminster John Knox, 2001), 225.
7. Oscar Wilde, "The Ballad of Reading Gaol," *Poets.org*, accessed August 16, 2014, http://www.poets.org/poetsorg/poem/ballad -reading-gaol.
8. Charles Spurgeon, "Love: A Sermon (No. 229)," *The Spurgeon Archive*, accessed August 15, 2014, http://www.spurgeon.org /sermons/0229.htm.
9. Martin Luther King Jr., *Strength to Love*, Fortress Press Gift Edition (Philadelphia: Fortress Press, 2010), 94.
10. Hippolytus of Rome, *Christian History: Quote of the Week*, posted April 5, 2007, accessed August 16, 2014, http://www .christianitytoday.com/ch/content/quote.html.
11. Emily Dickinson, "'Hope' is the thing with feathers," The Poems of Emily Dickinson, ed. R. W. Franklin (Cambridge: Harvard University Press, 1999), on Poetryfoundation.org, accessed August 15, 2014, http://www.poetryfoundation.org /poem/171619.

12. Frederick the Great, quoted in Rev. James Wood, compiler, *Dictionary of Quotations* (London: Frederick Warne and Co., 1893), 272.

DANCE PEACE GRACE FAITH
TIME LOVE GRATITU
HAPPINESS HOPE COMFOR
ACE WISDOM JOY GUIDANCE
MFORT LOVE TIME L
PEACE JOY HAPPINESS
LOVE
HAPPINESS GRACE WISD
GUIDANCE PEACE COMFO
GRATITUDE JOY FAI
GRACE HAPPINESS PEA
PE COMFORT HOPE GR
ISDOM GRACE GRATITUDE
TIME LOVE HAPPI
ATITUDE HOPE TIM
JOY LOVE TIME LOVE G
ACE HAPPINESS PEA
GRACE
GRATITUDE WISDOM JO
ISDOM FAITH JOY LOV
PEACE

DANCE PEACE GRACE FAITH
E TIME LOVE GRATITU
HAPPINESS HOPE COMFOR
ACE WISDOM JOY GUIDANC
MFORT LOVE TIME
PEACE JOY HAPPINES
LOVE
HAPPINESS GRACE WISD
GUIDANCE PEACE COMFO
Y GRATITUDE JOY FA
GRACE HAPPINESS PE
OPE COMFORT HOPE
E WISDOM GRACE GRATITUD
ACE TIME LOVE HAPP
GRATITUDE HOPE TI
HO
JOY LOVE TIME LOVE
PEACE HAPPINESS PEA
GRACE WISDOM J
H GRATITUDE JOY LO
ISDOM FAITH PEA